"After my thirty years as a Research Associate at Harvard's Fairbank Center for Chinese Studies, I can attest that Peter Wodtke is solidly in the top tier of Westerners who understand Chinese thinking, resentment, ambition, danger, and potential utility. America's tribal divisiveness today is suicidal, making us blind to, and therefore unable to survive intact the precarious and unpredictable years ahead of worldwide religious, economic , and military hostility, as climate change and global degradation and depletion inexorably advance. The book you are holding in your hands is a manual for survival. An agreement with China as partners, as brilliantly and persuasively proposed here, would be a giant enabler in escaping the grim "raft of the Medusa" future that is certain without it."

> *– Robert H. Morehouse, former Chairman, Atlas Copco K.K,*
> *and former President, Asian International Bank*

"Peter Wodtke's Everything to Gain is a brilliant and convincing blueprint for a new world order of peace and prosperity that is within our reach now, if reason, common sense, fiscal responsibility and a spirit of international cooperation are allowed to play the decisive role in determining our future. With calm, compelling judgment he surveys each region and nation, and suggests what steps are needed to put in place a world solution to equitable living on our planet. It should be read by every world leader, and by anyone who wants to think boldly and clearly about the future."

> *– Michael Korda, author of "Alone."*

"A unique analysis of world power, with particular emphasis on U.S., China, and Russia, and of issues not only from their respective histories, but also from their respective cultures, characters, and personalities of the people who run these countries, leading to a most valuable proposal and its knowhow for the purpose of avoiding possible catastrophe of humanity. This is based on vast and deep experience of the author who throughout his life worked in and with countries of many different cultures and histories. A very timely book which must be widely read by leaders and diplomats of the world."

> *– Makoto Yasuda, Former Chairman, Elders PICA Ltd., a*
> *leading multinational development investment firm in Asia.*

"Peter Wodtke has written an insightful and constructive review of the challenges now facing the US and the world, based partly on a close study of history and of recent events, partly on the author's practical business experience over many years in the countries he is writing about. Especially valuable at the present time is his analysis of the steps that are needed to put US-China relations on a stable footing; there is no more important task for policy makers in both countries and this book points the way forward."

— Geoffrey Owen, former editor of the Financial Times

"Peter Wodtke is one of the few global thought leaders — like a Henry Kissinger — who have spanned the decades, nations, and continents to speak with an insider's insight, a practitioner's practicality, and a scholar's intellect to address constructively the pressing global question from which everything else arguably hinges: the future of United States/China relations."

— David W. Miller, Ph.D., Princeton University, Director Faith & Work Initiative, Senior Professional Specialist, and Lecturer

EVERYTHING TO GAIN

China and the United States
as Future Partners

Author's Note

All my life I have been exposed to many cultures, that of New York City in the United States, where I was born in 1934; then Germany, France, Switzerland, and during my working life, Hong Kong, Japan, Southeast Asia, the Arab world, and the United Kingdom. I have always been a citizen of the United States, never a citizen of another country, though French people take me for being French, Germans take me for being German, and many take me for being Swiss.

My life is a history of global finance and business, including service multiple times as CEO, as chairman, and as a board member. I have a worldview, the experience of many cultures, and as a leader multiple times, I know how things get done right.

I step back from day-to-day electrifying news and media-created emotions and try to see what is going on and to observe trends in people, nations, technologies, cultures. I understand what Napoleon Bonaparte, Kaiser Wilhelm II, Vladimir Ilyich Lenin and Joseph Stalin, Adolf Hitler, Mao Zedong, Fidel Castro, and Ayatollah Ruhollah Khomeini did to their people and to the world.

In recent and contemporary times, the actions of Nicolás Maduro, Jair Bolsonaro, Teng Hsiao-p'ing, Vladimir Putin, Xi Jinping, Viktor Orbán, Kim Jong-Un, and Ayatollah Khamenei have reacted with prominent figures in the West like Angela Merkel, Emmanuel Macron, Barack Obama, Donald Trump, and Joe Biden.

Today's events are perilous.

The political posturing, the war in Ukraine, the standoff in the South China Sea over Taiwan, and terrifying weapons at the disposal of many countries can lead to accidental war and destruction of humankind.

If global nuclear war happens, climate change will be a nonevent.

In Europe, there were signs of repetition of the mistakes in judgment of Neville Chamberlain following his meeting with Adolf Hitler of Nazi Germany in 1938. The invasion of Ukraine was a startling wake-up call for Europe from a sleepy, comfortable, unreflective dependence on Russia for gas.

Yet Armageddon is not inevitable.

There are steps we can take to avoid it, bridges we can build to each other, political and military measures that can be taken to ensure proper behavior by nations and a sane world order that creates a context for people to live in safety and prosperity generations from now.

Peace and cooperation among nations will enable us to deal with climate change and with inequality.

This book is written from an American viewpoint, however one that has been influenced by the welcoming cultures of Asia, especially China and Japan, the Arab world, as well as Europe and the United Kingdom.

In the United States we argue among ourselves about gun control and about forgiving student loans when there are serious threats from potential adversaries abroad that have been growing in strength and ambition.

This book should encourage you to think about dangerous divisiveness in the United States and to make your own personal effort to move our country back to being a unified nation. That can be achieved by reaching out to other people, by tolerance of others, at first in your own community, then in your state and in our entire country.

If this book helps to prevent unintentional slide into the horror and abyss of war and moves us towards a better future, it will have done its job.

This book recommends unity inside the United States and a treaty of friendship and permanent peace between China and the United States, which Russia, the European Union, and all other countries will be invited to join.

Peter G. Wodtke
October 25, 2022

Table of Contents

TABLE OF CONTENTS

TABLE OF CONTENTS

Part VI: A new relationship between the United States and China

Preface

From the end of World War II on the United States has been the leading economic and military power in the world. Though that has changed gradually, as will be explained in Part II, "the United States", of this book, it has remained substantially true, though less so over time. The collapse of the Soviet Union, which was the second most important military power, in 1989 lent further support to the reality that the United States was the predominant power.

The terrorist attack on the World Trade Center and Pentagon of September 11, 2001, demonstrated that even the continental United States was vulnerable to a determined attack, and withdrawal from the Middle East in 2015, making way for our replacement by Russia and Iran, and the chaotic withdrawal from Afghanistan in 2021, demonstrated the limits of our leadership and of our dependability rather than a shortfall of military power.

For the most part United States leadership has been welcomed by nations that are themselves democracies. At times even allies have found United States policy frustrating, but given a choice, they have preferred to live with American leadership, hopefully being able to count on it, without American policy becoming prominent in their own backyards. America was trustworthy, considered with occasional cynicism, to "end up doing the right thing, after having tried everything else." Allies understood that the United States operated within a predictable policy range that worked well.

In the first two decades of this century, external actions, in particular by Russia and by China, started to change, and over time, changes became more noticeable and adversarial and in some instances went against long-standing American policies.

The United States now finds itself challenged on several fronts, largely as a result of our own lack of initiative, lack of follow-through, and preoccupation with domestic interests. Our American change of focus from a global view outside the United States to inside-the-country concerns resulted in a divided country domestically, a less competitive economy, and a far less effective actor on the global stage.

We face better organized international threats that we have not had to contend with before. *Everything to Gain* describes threatening issues the United States faces, and how we are facing, or in some cases, avoiding issues or allowing ourselves to be distracted from them.

Many issues are internal to the United States, but the destructive effect of the internal problems influence our relations with traditional allies as well as with Russia and China.

To survive as the nation and society we are, and to which we aspire in future, we must recognize the challenges we face and deal with them effectively.

Everything to Gain is a wake-up call for the nation, be it Republican or Democrat or apolitical, to make Americans aware of world events and their consequences for us.

Our leaders for the past two decades have been deficient in protecting the future of the United States and the American people.

Finding fault is easier than finding solutions, but there are solutions to many of our problems. Some problems require willingness to adapt and to change, and all of our problems would be far better managed with a unified nation, not a divided one.

Though *Everything to Gain* is primarily addressed to Americans, some of the issues described have their counterparts in other countries.

Americans are in this together, all 330 million of us. Each of us, young, middle-aged, and old have a stake in the future and want life to continue on a secure path. As I do myself, people care what happens to the United States, the American people, and their own lives and their descendants.

Many of the issues described in this book and the solutions proposed may be different from general perception of problems facing the United States.

Problems that we recognize as obvious need to be managed better, while others that are threatening are hardly perceived as dangers and must be recognized and dealt with.

Everything to Gain starts with two assumptions:

First assumption: that the United States exists in a competitive world.

PREFACE

"Competitive world" refers primarily to economic power, the impact of a productive society in terms of size of economy, productivity, cutting-edge technology and its continued development, and standard of living. It also includes image: the United States as a desirable example for other countries in its democracy and social impact, sometimes referred to as soft power, a society in which people enjoy honest elections, liberty and justice, care for others and a future for coming generations. Closely linked to economic power is military capability in defense and as an arm of national policy.

Second assumption: that a rival nation, China, aspires to become the dominant world economic and military power. Further, that another contender, seemingly an ally of China, Russia, desires in a nostalgic way, backed by military power, to recover the territory and influence enjoyed by its predecessor, the Soviet Union.

China "aspires to become" refers first to economic power, having the largest market serving a large population, producing goods and services of high quality and up-to-date technology at affordable prices, financing its economy through incoming investments and sales of exports with high world demand. China desires a harmonious world run on its terms. Following close behind economic power is buildup in military and naval strength and dedication to its centrally controlled system, which is called communist but is actually capitalist, with significant state actors in the economy.

Leading-edge technology is critical to success in the economy and in war, expanding political and economic and military reach around the globe and into space, as the dominant nation. "Aspires to become the dominant world power" invariably includes cutting-edge military power.

Russia "desires in a nostalgic way" refers to the sense that history is the driver for what Russia under Vladimir Putin would like as today's reality. Further, the vision of Mr. Putin is that it is up to present-day Russia to put matters right. Russia wants to recover the territory and influence that was lost with the crash of Soviet communism, and more distantly back, under Russia's Tsar Peter the Great and Tsarina Catherine the Great.

An important aspect is that China and Russia are both autocracies. Their leaders, Xi Jinping and Vladimir Putin, had in one of their periodic meetings in February 2022 pledged friendship to each other in pursuit of their common interests. Those interests as they perceive them particularly include erosion of the United States' historical position as the leader of the free world.

If the first assumption about a competitive world is true, and the second assumption about the rise of China to be the dominant power is true, are these assumptions threatening to the United States as well as to countries around the world allied to the United States?

My view on the first assumption is we are indeed in a competitive world and that it is vital to maintain our global economic competitiveness at today's level, improve it on the military front, and exercise better leadership.

This book discusses issues affecting our competitive standing and whether or not we are acting in a manner that will maintain or enhance our global competitive position.

If we desire to remain globally competitive our president, administration, and Congress as well as the American people need to look at ourselves, examine our situation and our performance, and evaluate whether we are maintaining the status quo of our global competitive position or whether we are slipping behind.

An analysis has to examine our economic position, our education, our productivity, our military capability, and our social power, including our image among the world's nations.

If we are living in a competitive world and we find shortcomings in how we are maintaining our competitiveness, what must we do to improve?

The second assumption concerning China and Russia is threatening to the United States and to our future. We must be aware of the issues and of the threats. We have to act to protect our status and avoid an unintentional slide into war.

The reality of each of these two assumptions will return throughout this book. As we look at issues confronting our nation. Part V is about a new approach to the future and recommends what we as a nation can and should do about the challenges we face.

Part VI recommends a proactive engagement with China for a new world order. Instead of seeking to protect ourselves against China and to contain China, we should look at the great opportunity for the United States and China reaching out to each other and entering a new relationship of friendship and permanent peace.

The objective of this book is, in light of the two assumptions and the issues we face, to end up with answers to the following questions:

What must we do to ensure that the United States maintain and improve our competitive position in the world?

What would be the elements of a treaty of friendship and permanent peace between China and the United States? How would such a treaty be good for China, America, and the world?

Part I:
The Contenders Against Pax Americana

CHAPTER 1

Russia – where experience, autocracy, and nostalgia meet

Russia is discussed first, because – though a lesser power than China or the United States – it is the perpetrator of the largest war since the end of World War II, a deliberate attack on an innocent nation, Ukraine.

The magnificent civilization of Russia, writings by Dostoyevsky, Tolstoy, Gogol, Chekhov, Pushkin, Maxim Gorky, and music by Tchaikovsky, Scriabin, Rimsky-Korsakov, Borodin, Stravinsky, Prokofiev, too numerous to mention are found in educated homes in every corner of the globe, a constant reminder to we who enjoy them of the richness and variety and humanity of Russia and its history.

Deeply cultured with a long history, far longer than that of the USA but much shorter than that of China, Russia has a tradition of autocratic rule and rough and violent treatment towards its nobles and its humble people from rulers like Ivan the Terrible, Peter the Great, Catherine the Great, Nicholas II, and in the twentieth-century Joseph Stalin.

Geographically Russia is the largest country, much larger in area even than Canada. However, Russia has an overall population of 144 million compared to the 330 million of the United States, the 1.4 billion of China, and the 1.4 billion of India..

Heavily armed since World War II throughout Soviet times, its military power refreshed in recent years under Vladimir Putin, Russia is a provider of weaponry to itself and other countries. In possession of the atomic bomb, the hydrogen bomb, and the neutron bomb, Russia's large military commitment is driven by an ingrained sense from generation to generation that it has to defend itself and to assert global influence following invasions of Russia by Sweden in 1707, by Napoleon Bonaparte in 1812, and by Adolf Hitler's Nazi Germany in 1941, on the heels of the German Soviet Non-Aggression Pact of 1939.

CHAPTER 1

Russia lived through foreign invasions and has paid terrible costs, successfully repelling invaders who suffered staggering losses. The invasion of Russia by the army of Napoleon Bonaparte started with some 680,000 soldiers of which only 27,000 survived disease, brutal Russian winter, and battles with the Russian army. Three armies of Nazi Germany invaded Russia with 3,000,000 soldiers of which nearly that entire number were killed, wounded, or taken prisoner over the years of the war. Russia itself lost 18,000,000 soldiers and civilians during World War II, most connected to the Nazi invasion, a staggering figure that continues to be present in the minds of Russians through the generations.

Embedded in the culture of the country is deep paranoia, the feeling that Russia is not liked in the West and must move with strength and cleverness to promote its advantage and to survive. In its own mind, Russia is always under threat and if one looks back at history from a Russian viewpoint, the invasions of 1707, 1812, and 1941 prove it.

"Not liked in the West" is a well-grounded feeling that has been periodically refreshed, in 1945 and afterwards by the grasping behavior of Stalin and the Soviet Union throughout Eastern Europe, by the blockade of Berlin in 1946, the attack on Georgia in 2008, the illegal seizure of Crimea in 2014, and on February 24, 2022, through Russia's massive assault in February 2022 on the independent country of Ukraine.

Based on experience the Russian state is feared abroad, underlined by the reality that the Russian people themselves had only a few years of freedom in the 1990s, and that since then, the control of the state on behavior and thought of Russian citizens has become gradually stronger, to the point where in 2022 there is no opposition possible to the regime without risking severe punishment.

Russia's largest geographic reach was under the Soviet Union, and the late Mikhail Gorbachev, Party leader in the 1980s, has never been forgiven by some Russians for *glasnost* (openness) and *perestroika* (reform). The gradual relaxation of political control under Gorbachev led to exodus of people from Soviet-controlled East Germany, the fall of the Berlin Wall in 1989, the unification of West and East Germany in 1990, and the disintegration of the Soviet Union itself in December 1991, which followed the declaration of three of the Soviet republics, notably including Russia itself and Ukraine, that the Soviet Union no longer existed.

During the years of the Soviet Union from 1917 to 1991 the economy was under government central control in a planned economy and local control for execution and implementation. The government was controlled by members of the Communist Party, bureaucrats, and employees. Political opponents, including those of high rank, were exiled to Siberia or tried, convicted, and executed.

The private economy came alive after the 1991 disintegration of the Soviet Union. Certain bureaucrats with insights and the right connections appropriated to themselves huge parts of the previously government-controlled economy. This gained them enormous personal fortunes corruptly, the individuals doing this becoming known as oligarchs.

Gradually private businesses extending services and manufacturing consumer products offered choice to consumers. Over time shortages and lack of choice characteristic of the Soviet Union ended.

The freest years of the new, post-1991 Russia were during the 1990s under Boris Yeltsin, when the institutions that today govern Russia were new and untried, an unbridled atmosphere that calmed down after a while. Boris Yeltsin was president from 1991 to 1999, when he resigned and was succeeded by Vladimir Putin, the president now. Russia has had only two presidents in the space of thirty years, and President Putin is likely to stay in power for years to come.

There is no evident competitor to Putin. Profiled opposition candidates like Alexei Navalny end up poisoned or in prison. Many of the oligarchs became seriously rich; some emigrated to Britain and other countries like the United Arab Emirates. Some stayed, in particular associates who benefited from the benevolence of Putin and who helped to enrich him. Ambitious persons running counter to Putin, like Mikhail Khodorkovsky, who served ten years in prison, found that opposing Putin carries a heavy price.

Putin, like his predecessors Catherine the Great and Joseph Stalin, is infused with the dream of the Russian empire. Putin wrote a 5,000-word essay on July

CHAPTER 1

12, 2021, setting out his imperial vision on the historical unity of Russians and Ukrainians.

That essay is worth reading. It is written with academic flavor, providing historical facts going back hundreds of years, presented from the Russian point of view. It is a statement of complaints by Putin about "anti-Russian" moves by the West, allegations that Ukraine is influenced by Nazis, and the intention of Putin to reincorporate Ukraine into Russia on the basis of common ethnology, history, language, and culture.

Anything short of integration of Ukraine into Russia is depicted as an offense to the Ukrainian people and is surrender to Western intrigue. Among the interesting points in the essay, Putin is highly critical of the Bolsheviks and the Soviet Union for its assignment of borders to peoples and states within the Soviet Union, which he felt laid the basis for future problems. This essay gave advance notice of Putin's intention to invade Ukraine in February 2022, and the vast accumulation of weaponry on the Ukraine border starting in late 2021 was the fighting force to execute it.

Putin repeatedly says that the collapse of the Soviet Union is the "greatest tragedy in the history of the world," demonstrating his nostalgia for the past.

If the post–World War II Soviet Union were reconstructed, it would include Moldova, Ukraine, Armenia, Georgia, Azerbaijan, Turkmenistan, Uzbekistan, Tajikistan, Kazakhstan, Lithuania, Latvia, and Estonia with working control over the politics and economies of Poland, Czechoslovakia, Hungary, Romania, Bulgaria, eastern Germany and all of the Balkans, many of which are now part of the European Union and some of which are members of NATO.

If one looks at it as Putin sees it in terms of lost populations, lost territory, and lost influence from 1991 to the present, it is a terrible loss, an unbearable shrinkage.

Vladimir Putin wants to recover it and he is prepared to use as much force as necessary to accomplish what he wants.

This works out as a game of chess, in which Russians excel. Plan ahead, build strength, threaten, take two steps forward and one back, bluff and fool the opposition as to your next move. Russia intervened in Georgia in 2008, it seized Crimea from Ukraine in 2014, the world complained, but no country took steps to undo the steal and recover Crimea.

Russia then incited/encouraged disorders in eastern Ukraine, Donetsk and Luhansk, the most culturally Russian part of the country while the western part went through an "Orange" revolution and deposed Kremlin sympathetic president Yanukovych, a move opposite to what the Kremlin wanted. A politically independent Ukraine was a setback to Putin's dreams of rebuilding the Russian empire.

In 2020 Russia supported strongman Lukashenko in dishonest Belarus elections, thus cementing Russian influence in the country bordering Poland, Lithuania, and Ukraine. All these internationally illegal and morally improper moves cost Putin little.

An irritant to Putin is that most of the population of Ukraine, including many in the culturally Russian eastern part, sees its future as connected to the West, in terms of free elections, possible association some day with the European Union, even possible membership of NATO.

Faced with the Russian military buildup on their border in late 2021 and 2022 and the attack that started February 24, 2022, Ukrainians have fought hard. With great destruction of cities, people, and livelihoods Russia captured Mariupol and the Sea of Azov and made great inroads in eastern Ukraine, ensuring an unbroken line of Russian control from Crimea through the Sea of Azov to Donetsk and Luhansk. Russia is resorting to shelling civilian areas and communications, causing great hardship and much loss of life, a revival of medieval attacks on populations.

As of October 2022, the outcome is undecided but lately the Ukrainians, using French long-range howitzers and American HIMARS long-distance artillery, have made very significant gains. Russia has called up its reserves and has reintroduced conscription. Reservists are being given a two-week refresher course before being sent in to combat.

Russian military deaths will be unpopular in Russia, not least that the Russian armies lined up on the borders of Ukraine were told that they were there simply for maneuvers, not for a real-life assault on another country. That the attack on Ukraine did not succeed in forty-eight hours was a most unwelcome surprise to Putin, who greatly overestimated how the Russian attack would overwhelm Ukraine.

The Russian economy has never been strong in the export of Russian manufactured goods, but Russia is an exporter of minerals and of oil and gas to Europe, a critical need for Europe giving rise to stress over the North Sea pipeline, which would be immensely useful to Europe as a source of gas if operational but has now been shut down, causing a shortage of natural gas in Europe and rationing for users, as well as an urgent search for new supplies.

Unlike many over-borrowed Western countries, the finances of Russia have been properly managed up until the Russian attack on Ukraine, following which there was a collapse of the value of the Russian ruble and a rush by ordinary Russians to convert their rubles into – of all things – US one-hundred-dollar notes, thus demonstrating that despite the crazy adventure of the Russian leadership in attacking Ukraine, individual citizens understood what was good for them.

Putin has been adept at building his control of Russia within the framework of the written constitution. When he had served two terms as president by the year 2007, he exchanged places with his prime minister appointee Dmitry Medvedev, who became president for four years until Putin became eligible to run for president again in 2011. Medvedev eventually resigned and in 2020 the prime minister became Mikhail Mishustin, who had run the tax service. Putin remained in charge throughout. The view and ambitions of Putin matter; his ambitions are those of Russia for the time being and for his lifetime.

Although he sees the world in terms of the Russian empire, Putin does not see the world in ideological terms; he has no regrets about the disappearance of communism and no interest in proselytizing communism. What Putin gained from Soviet Communism was single-person rule at the top. Putin sometimes uses Christian allusions in his talks, therefore supporting the Russian Orthodox church, which he sees as a source of favorable, pro-Russian influence in other Christian countries.

CHAPTER 1

Putin sees the world in terms of historical experience at the hands of foreign invaders, an economy that has potential and can project power, restoration of the territory of the Soviet Union, and a twenty-first-century version of global influence, adapted to the needs of Russia and the realities of technology and the situations of other countries, some of which are potential adversaries.

Looking at the situation from Putin's standpoint, one can see why he considers the expansion of the European Union and NATO as threatening, less from a military standpoint as from yearning for freedom, independence, and honest elections in "color" revolutions in countries like Georgia and Ukraine that he sees as part of the historical Russian empire. Unless such activity is stopped, freedom and free elections could spread to countries like Belarus, immediately to the west of Russia, and to Russia itself.

In summary, Putin sees the Russia he runs as unfinished business that necessitates taking calculated risks in order to grasp what he sees as obvious opportunities to restore might and reach. That said, Putin cannot afford to lose the support of the Russian people; Russia has elections, however carefully overseen, and Putin is in power by right and not by might. The structure is in place so that at election time the Russian people have to be satisfied with how the country is run.

Putin's ambitions for the restoration of the Russian empire are "top down," and to some extent also "bottom up," especially in the minds and recollections of older people who remember the extent and armed might of the Soviet Union. What younger Russian people want is a better life, a secure and promising future, and connection with the world outside. Restoration of empire is low on their list, but if it is done with minimal risk in Russian lives and with a gain in prestige they are supportive and will credit Putin for the victory.

There is a long cultural tradition in Russia that the Tsar is a father figure, that he looks after his people and their needs, that his judgment is inherently good and benefits the country. During periods when people felt oppressed such as during the reigns of Catherine the Great and of Nicholas II there was resistance.

Putin benefits from this many centuries' old cultural heritage and tradition, in that older people may give him the benefit of the doubt and believe that he is doing the right thing for Russia in seeking to reintegrate Ukraine into Russia with force. Therefore, there is passive cultural support within Russia for the invasion of Ukraine.

Following the invasion of Ukraine European countries, the USA, the United Kingdom, Australia, and Japan have heavily sanctioned Russia, some Russian companies, and Foreign Minister Lavrov and Putin personally, their inner ruling circle as well as the profiled "oligarchs" who depend on assets and connections in the West. Russia became, from a respected member and trade participant in the family of nations, a pariah state in the space of a week.

There are significant dangers ahead: firstly for the Ukrainian people, who are dying and suffering, the enormous destruction in the country, the vast disruption of food and commodity exports from Ukraine and corresponding loss of income, and displacement of over two and a half million people leaving the country and fleeing to Moldova, to Poland, to Hungary.

A threatening aspect for its neighbors is growing closeness between Russia and Belarus and the stationing of Russian troops in Belarus. That positions Russian troops on the frontier of Poland, Lithuania, and Latvia, all countries that are now members of NATO and all territories within the former Soviet sphere of influence or actually part of the Soviet Union.

Lithuania and Poland have the further problem that the Kaliningrad Oblast, formerly Koenigsberg (Germany), is a permanent part of Russia, hundreds of miles from the Russian border; to access it from Russia one has to pass through Poland or Lithuania, EU members and NATO members. In the mood Putin is at present, Russian troops in Belarus coming up against NATO troops in Poland and Lithuania, the likelihood of dangerous posturing and a possible mishap is enhanced.

For Russians at home the invasion of Ukraine has been a disaster: a 25 percent fall in the value of the ruble, which later partially recovered, shrinkage of the economy, likely recession and fall in the standard of living together with deaths and wounding of thousands of Russian soldiers. For Putin, a bad surprise that his army did not perform as expected, crippling sanctions, and a devastating loss of prestige for Putin and for Russia. With all that has happened, Putin's anger and frustration has grown, which increases the risk that this unpredictable autocrat may take violent nuclear or biological warfare action against Ukraine or against western European countries, especially those on Russia's border.

Add to this a statement that Russian State TV presenter Dmitry Kiselyov made on February 28, 2022, after the invasion of Ukraine on February 24: "Why do we need a world if Russia is not in it?" That should cause every one of the six billion of us on earth to think about it, to judge the statement, and consider the consequences: no world unless Russia gets its way. Since February 2022 Putin has been constantly hardening his use of the oil weapon against western Europe, hoping to create misery when cold weather sets in. In his creation of misery elsewhere, Putin plays a weak hand with skill.

Despite the adeptness of Mr. Putin in the difficult circumstances in which he finds himself, the actions of Russia in Ukraine have done lasting damage to Russia's reputation in the world. Irrespective of the outcome of the war on Ukraine, Russia will be treated with great caution in the years ahead.

CHAPTER 2

China - The time is now

The millennium that began in the year 2000 is China's millennium.

It is the time when the long history of over 4,000 years, the ingrained culture that is deeply within Chinese, the experiences with different kinds of rulers and systems, the contacts with foreign powers during the past thousand years, will all be gathered together as a base for the future of its people and to have an indelible impression on the world.

It was Napoleon Bonaparte who said, "China is a sleeping giant. Let her sleep, for when she wakes, she will shake the world," understanding that if this huge country of intelligent and hardworking people woke up from its slumbers it could dominate the earth. That waking up has been happening since 1949, more so after the death of Mao Zedong in 1976.

What is different about China?

Most people everywhere, given a chance, will choose work over idleness, and it is human nature to work hard to establish a position in life, to put a roof over one's head, to feed a family, and to seek a future for one's children.

In these qualities Chinese people are exceptional. Chinese are hardworking, resourceful, ingenious, smiling and many Chinese have another quality that not all of us on this earth share: ingrained optimism. Chinese people often believe that through their own hard work things can be made better, that suffering and hardship are temporary, possibly only for the current generation, and that it's possible to find solutions.

Seeing an expensive car go by, a Chinese may think, "if I work hard and I am fortunate, maybe someday I can afford that car, and if I cannot, maybe my children will be able to afford that car." Thinking this way is a source of strength.

The fortitude of hundreds of millions of Chinese as individuals has enabled China to live through millennia of poverty, of oppressive government for long periods of time, of disease, of famine and emerge with a positive attitude about possibilities for the future. Chinese people feel the history and culture of their ancient race, 4,000 and more years of history, and this feeling contributes to assurance that they will prevail.

Thousands of years of history teach endurance, and the experience of history shows that difficulties are temporary and can be overcome, likely only in generations to come. Oppressive government will come and will go away. Gratification is understood as not coming at once, not in a year, possibly not in a person's lifetime but possible and even probable in succeeding generations.

The ability to postpone gratification is an enormous source of strength. We in the West consider it patience on the part of China, but it is not actually patience. Chinese are no more patient than other people and often less so. The ability to defer gratification reflects a sense of their history. It is not patience, it is cultural self-confidence.

There is no other people on earth who have a generalized feeling that things can be made better, and that ills, no matter how damaging, destructive, and hurtful, are temporary. If individuals suffer and pass away, the Chinese people live on.

In such a culture, mere days, weeks, years, and one's own lifetime reflect a measured sense of proportion. Improvement can be in small steps, minuscule, but improvements come and they are noted and celebrated, though they are only stages to the next step in improvement. In China the structure of a ruling system is secondary to the energy, enthusiasm, and optimism of the individual.

Fifty years ago China under Mao Zedong suffered famines, terrible oppression, loss of education by millions of young people sent to work in deserts and on farms in order to break bourgeois habits.

A generation suffered but the next generation broke the curse; Teng Hsiao-p'ing encouraged constructive, individually driven work and entrepreneurship; he was the liberator of the Chinese people. Under Teng, people worked for themselves, provided themselves with basic needs, gradually achieved personal security and a taste of and longing for the good life.

China became more prosperous; people became used to a better life and wanted it to continue. Increasingly Chinese people wanted freedom, a natural desire of every human, but in a *dirigiste* state there were limits. The freedom demonstrations in Tiananmen Square, Beijing, in 1989 were brutally put down.

Teng Hsiao-p'ing is the unsung hero of China in 2022. The end of Mao's cultural revolution brought freedom to hundreds of millions of people in that people were encouraged to work for themselves and for their families. Freedom after the Cultural Revolution unleased capacities of hundreds of millions of people and the return to high-quality education.

Encouragement from the top changed China from a large but poor, highly regulated country at the end of the life of Mao Zedong in 1976 into the economic powerhouse that it is today: a leading technology center as well as the world's manufacturing leader.

What it took was economic freedom, hard work, optimism, and a great deal of imported technology. China became in a few decades a business country where every company wanted to be. A vast amount of technology was introduced into China by European, Japanese, and American companies, and in huge measure that technology was transferred to local Chinese individuals and to Chinese businesses.

Add to that the learning of millions of Chinese people studying overseas in universities in Europe and North America, combined with the eagerness to learn and drive to excel in studies, and the consequent return of technology from overseas home, and it is easy to see why China became the number two global economy in less than two generations.

Technology transfer is vastly easier than it was in the time of Mao Zedong. Chinese and others from developing countries were educated in the West and Japan, went to work for foreign companies, and learned the science and technology to compete. Not content to copy, China and Chinese have taken modern technology and developed it further in digitization, data manipulation, manufacturing, and artificial intelligence, as well as espionage, warfare, and cyber-warfare.

CHAPTER 2

China has deep-rooted ambitions to undo the humiliations it suffered at the hands of Western countries during the Opium Wars of the 1840s and the time of foreign colonies inside China. The weakness of the Qing Dynasty was evident for years and ended under the leadership of Dr. Sun Yat-sen in 1912, first president of the Republic of China.

Chinese historical ambitions are deeply rooted in Xi Jinping, president of China since 2013 and secretary-general of the Chinese Communist Party. Xi is the self-appointed vehicle for China's latent ambitions whose time has come.

There is a match between the sense prevailing among Chinese people and the desire of Xi to be the instrument that realizes it. With time Xi has gathered more power to himself, starting with replacing a grayer, less noteworthy figure, Hu Jintao, the predecessor of Xi. From the start of his appointment there was no political competition that Xi could not overcome.

Under Hu Jintao, Chinese had become wealthier. China was moving forward as the manufacturer to the world, but there was little advancement in terms of national prestige and no progress of note on redressing the humiliations of the past in the eyes of Chinese.

Xi's route was twofold: he gained internal power by the drive to eliminate corruption, which drive was tilted towards persons that were potential rivals to the future power of Xi. Persons such as the highly profiled mayor of Chongqing are in prison and have disappeared from public view. They will never be seen again: a double benefit, as potential rivals to Xi have been eliminated and what happened to them is not lost on persons with political ambitions, who have seen that it is dangerous to cross Xi.

China grew and prospered from 2013 to 2020. Much of the prosperity came from the remarkable growth and dynamism of the Chinese economy exemplified by companies like Jack Ma's Ant and Alibaba and Pony Ma's Tencent. Some of these multibillionaires had ambitions of political influence but failed to consider patterns in their own Chinese history and to understand the limitations of their own influence in the face of Xi.

Xi cut them down to size in short order, with a few strokes reducing their influence, controlling their ability to gather support in foreign countries, and put ambitious billionaires under great personal pressure, bringing those that are still visible to heel.

There is latent interest in democracy in China, an inevitable result of much broader and better education since the time of Mao Zedong, and an amazing rise in the standard of living, first in the cities but increasingly spreading to the expanded cities and the country side. Yet democracy will not happen in the foreseeable future; there is no structure or means for it to happen in a one-party state where any candidates for office have to be officially approved.

Unlike many other countries, China would perform economically much the same as a democracy and as a business-inclined communist state that encouraged economic freedom; the real strength is that of the Chinese people and not that of the system.

From the start of communist rule in 1949 China has been a surveillance society, where perceived antisocial behavior, especially deviation from political orthodoxy, was reported to authorities by government-appointed informers in organizations, schools, and neighborhoods. In recent decades the advance of technology has made surveillance easier, universal, and has taken the "local" out of surveillance, thereby eliminating a source of bias by an informer who didn't like someone in the community.

Electronic surveillance has increasingly uniform application, for example in access to credit, to schooling, to party membership, and all kinds of privilege as well as punishment for bad behavior, as defined from time to time. China is a country where, increasingly, everything is known about everyone and recorded, but access to this information on people is highly stratified, itself a matter of privilege, with Xi probably the only individual in China with access to everything on everyone.

In the technological age, behavior is monitored by exception, dots are connected when specific kinds of behavior are related to each other and to facial recognition. China is not a country where there is rule of law in the Western sense; people may be detained without specific accusations against them and without trial, and if there are trials they may be held without outside witnesses and without media in attendance.

Increasingly so in years to come, electronically monitored behavior will be the key to access, to privilege, to inclusion and exclusion, and to punishment in China. The technology is in hand and has been partially deployed, with more to come. Paradoxically, extreme surveillance may give rise to disobedience when enough well-connected people feel the same way. As long as ruling authorities have control it is not an issue. The harvest of electronic information will be very carefully analyzed in China and will be used for the purposes of the leadership in control.

Internationally China followed a new path, the "belt and road initiative," a modern Silk Road connecting China with the nations of central Asia, Africa, and Europe, as well as a maritime silk road greatly expanding China's trading and naval presence throughout the world to include Africa and Latin America. As this has evolved it has given rise to complaints of useless prestige projects, corruption, work being done by imported labor from China instead of local people, and overindebtedness of countries on harsh repayment terms, in all a growing amount of hard feeling against China. Still, many projects have been economically beneficial to recipient countries at a time when the United States and other Western countries took insufficient initiatives in transfer of technology to emerging countries and did not make funding available. China stepped into the breach, with some gain in prestige and some blame, a mixed blessing.

Moving west from China, there are Chinese naval bases in Cambodia, Myanmar, Pakistan, Djibouti, the UAE, Tanzania, and Equatorial Guinea on the Atlantic Coast.

In the Western hemisphere China has become a supporter of the Maduro regime in Venezuela, which is devastating for its own people but a useful irritant to the United States in its violation of the 1823 Monroe Doctrine, in the Pacific on the island of Kiribati, and potentially in the Solomon Islands. Many, but not all, of the countries China supports have autocratic leadership, which does not do well with democracy, so there is implicit understanding between these countries and China. Some client countries, such as Greece, a dynamic democracy, have had second thoughts, wishing that they had not accepted China's offered development funds and loans so mindlessly.

CHAPTER 2

With little fanfare, China's military and navy have undergone rapid expansion. Looking at a map of the world, the locations of Chinese naval bases effectively surround the United States, which in recent years, now has the world's second largest navy compared to that of China, which is now the largest.

China is different from the pre-1991 communist Soviet Union, different in its people and how it engages with the world. It is a resourceful society of hardworking people. It is a natural environment in which to create new ways of doing things, improved applications, especially technological improvements on how things are done in the West.

Unlike Russia, China has no yearning to be culturally accepted by the West.

China is dynamic, inventive, growing, expanding outward. For the first time in history China overcame natural barriers to communication and travel and created a remarkable network of rail, road, and air connections. Each part of China knows what is going on in the other parts, modern Internet technology, virtual private networks, and the highly developed surveillance system make it impossible for one part of the country to break out of the nation.

With vigor and perseverance China has insisted on the adoption of Mandarin, the national language, and has simplified the written language from around 12,000 Chinese characters to around 3,000 to 4,000. Those are phenomenal achievements in pulling a people and diverse regions, each with its dialect, together.

China is developing important technology of its own, no doubt in part seeded by discoveries and in some cases intellectual theft from the West, but the furtherance of technology and its application in practice has led to enormous wealth for hundreds of Chinese entrepreneurs and a vast increase in living standards in China.

Many new technologies will have great implications for the betterment of lives of the Chinese people. Despite lip service to care for the environment, China will put its economic interests first, especially in access to and processing of raw materials and the employment of fossil fuels and nuclear power. When needed, China will make pleasant noises to satisfy the demands in the short term of ESG; what actually happens will be in China's best interests as China sees them.

CHAPTER 2

There is too much at stake for the 1.4 billion energetic people of China for the Chinese economic and nationalism machine to slow down in the medium term. Short term, the political restrictions that Xi has placed on industries that he felt were growing too powerful or that were started to be negative influences, as he saw them, on society or billionaires that were growing too self-important, together with massive overinvestment and overborrowing in real estate have slowed the growth of the economy. The slowdown will be temporary.

Xi cut the billionaires down to size, thereby showing his political might while directing the economy into moralistic paths that he personally approved.

Reading translations of the writings of upper management in China shows that ministers under Xi spend time interpreting his wishes and may be personally at risk if they are wrong. China is moving strongly under Xi in the direction of one-person rule.

During the past two years Xi's measures have slowed down development of the economy, have created personal discomfort and inconvenience in China through his strict, anti-Covid lockdown measures, and possibly terminal constraints to the highly productive, free economy of Hong Kong through the passage of the Security Law.

China is too dynamic and too intimately connected with the rest of the world to untie the economic and financial connections that exist, that benefit China and also benefit the countries and peoples in the exchange of goods and services with China. Business and development may benefit China more, but there is benefit for the other side as well. With the caveat of Xi's measures in the past two years, China is on a roll.

China does not see its own role in the world as aggressive. China seeks to promote harmony among nations, which could be seen as peace and nonaggression among the nations of the world on China's terms. China does not want to attack anyone, and its military buildup is not intended to be a tool for aggression but to be able to enforce China's vision of global harmony.

There are many locations where the Chinese vision of harmony comes up against a different vision, notably that of the United States and its allies including Japan and Australia. Those locations include Taiwan, the Pacific

Islands, the South China Sea, and the Sea of Japan, Southeast Asia, especially Cambodia and Thailand, parts of central Asia, parts of Africa, and Venezuela and Nicaragua and El Salvador, as well as, potentially, the Antarctic and the Arctic. There are indeed many parts of the world where the Chinese vision of harmony, backed by Chinese military and naval reach, comes up against the interests of western Europe, Japan, Australia, India, and New Zealand, plenty of opportunities for potential conflict.

Xi Jinping sees the United States as China's rival, however a rival about which little has to be done: time and dynamism and the idea of harmony are on China's side, in the same time frame as the United States is harming itself with its inward focus and deep internal divisions.

If seriously challenged by the United States, China will work to turn the financial system of the world to its advantage and to the detriment of the United States. This is China's least discussed goal, biding its time, and will be enlarged on in this book.

International containment of China, led by the United States, will not work.

Containment of the Soviet Union worked because miliary power was well matched, and war would have resulted in mutually assured destruction. Militarily, Russia was a giant, and in certain countries there was theoretical admiration of the communist system as Russia practiced it, but economically Russia was never an important global player.

China is a different story. With a far larger population than any country except India, cutting-edge economic technology, and an economy deeply integrated with the rest of the world, very much including the United States, in recent years China has built the world's largest navy and a powerful air force and missile force. With such deep integration into the world economy backed by a powerful military, where would containment start? It is not possible, except in very small and ineffective measures, for containment of China to start in the economy or international trade.

If containment is not possible, China and the United States have to find a *modus vivendi*, a way to live together.

CHAPTER 2

The United States will have to adapt its situation and its mentality to live with a China that will be the world's most important economic player. That will require an adjustment to a new world in which the United States becomes the second most important power.

The relationship between the United States and China deteriorated in the past several years. Increased aggressiveness on the part of Xi, whom President Trump admired as a person but whose admiration did the United States no good. It deteriorated further during the Biden administration.

Growing confidence on the part of the Chinese military and focus on the United States as the potential adversary, harsh security measures taken in Hong Kong, warming of ties between Russia and China, and increased overflights of Taiwan airspace by the Chinese air force each contributed to deterioration of the China/USA relationship.

From the USA side, finger-pointing about the origin of Covid, reporting of alleged theft of information from American companies and universities, increased defense measures aimed at curbing China in concert with the United Kingdom, Australia, and Japan, and to some extent India, censuring of Huawei and selective other Chinese companies, and controls on strategic exports from the USA to China all contributed to deterioration.

The flashpoint of an armed conflict is most likely to be over Taiwan, and China will be watching Western and USA behavior in regard to Russia's attack on Ukraine.

If Russian aggression is successful, with little redress from the West except for sanctions, and gradual loss of interest by the West in Ukraine or fear by the West that Russia may use nuclear weapons, China may judge that the time is right to take back Taiwan by force. If things go that far, it will be extremely difficult to avoid war.

The tipping point in favor of a modicum of stability may be China's own present economic problems and the example the Ukrainian people have set in resisting the invasion by Russia, which is certainly food for thought, even in China.

CHAPTER 2

Ukraine has put up fierce resistance to Russian attack. The Ukrainian government remains in place and a source of inspiration to its military; Xi seems to have been surprised that Putin actually attacked Ukraine as it is possible that he was not told when the two leaders met in Beijing on February 5.

That was one surprise; the second was that the huge Russian army has not prevailed. Xi may have sharpened his view of Putin and quietly, privately, may be backing off the "best friend" relationship announced on February 5, 2022.

November 2022 will see the reappointment of Xi Jinping for a third term as Party General Secretary. The time till November 2022 is likely to be calm, despite events seen as inflammatory as the visit to Taiwan in August by Nancy Pelosi, Speaker of the US House of Representatives.

After November 2022, when Xi Jinping is reappointed, events could become highly unpredictable, but also a time of opportunity for a new relationship. The USA, China's neighbors, and the West need to be prepared for all eventualities.

CHAPTER 3

China–Russia cooperation

The primary political objective of China–Russia cooperation is to displace American dominant influence on global events and to undo relationships that the United States has with countries around the world, especially countries of the emerging markets.

Comparing China with Russia, China's global ambitions are substantially "bottom up," broadly shared by the Chinese people, augmented by powerful "top down" leadership, as compared to largely "top down" ambitions of Putin for Russia.

Chinese people feel that "their time has come"; there is no comparable feeling among ordinary Russians. China's ambitions are broader, general, cultural, in comparison to which the ambitions of Russia, while large in desire for geography and recovery of influence, are limited, definable, driven by Putin.

Older Russians often share the nostalgia of Putin for the size and influence of the Soviet Union. Middle-class Russians are more likely to believe that the primary task of their leadership is to improve the economy and to create a better life.

Chinese do not think this way because they know their economy has already made vast strides benefiting much of Chinese society and are confident it can move ahead farther. The middle class in China does not necessarily share the wish of Xi Jinping to contain America, as many Chinese have relatives in the United States and Canada, students in schools and universities in the USA and the West, and for many, an out-of-sight nest egg in the United States in the form of an apartment or house or land.

The two economies are vastly different in their global reach, China's being so much larger and far more dynamic. China's population is nine times the size of that of Russia. China can manage economically without Russia, and Russia is the "junior partner" in the China–Russia cooperation. Conversely, the support of China is critically important to Russia.

CHAPTER 3

In light of Russia's lack of early success in overcoming Ukraine and condemnation of Russia in addition to Western sanctions, the relationship will increasingly be on China's terms. Between the two countries there will be no pretense of equality.

Cooperation of recent years between Russia and China is a marriage of convenience and not a marriage of love. Throughout history feeling between the two countries has been adversarial and not friendly. During Stalinist times there was a period of years, 1962 to the late 1970s, when the two communist countries severed their relationship.

Xi Jinping sees opportunities in cooperation with Russia in joint naval exercises in the area of China's single most important territorial expansion ambition, the Nine Dash Line in the South China Sea.

Claim to a "Nine Dash Line" was made by the Republic of China (now situated in Taiwan) in 1947, first as an "eleven dash line," reduced to a nine dash line in 1949 when the Communists took over China and the Nationalists retreated to Taiwan.

The "Nine Dash Line" is a claim to purported historic rights in a very large area of the South China Sea, covering maritime areas claimed in part by the Philippines, Vietnam, and Malaysia and, very significantly, including the sea routes from Southeast Asia to Japan and Korea.

The Philippines in 2013 brought a lawsuit against China for its claim to the maritime territory of the nine dash line, and in 2016 an arbitration tribunal in the Hague ruled that China had no lawful basis to claim the maritime territory of the nine dash line under the United Nations Convention on the Law of the Sea.

Neither China nor Taiwan took part in the arbitration and both rejected its findings.

In 2022 there remain critical contested interests within the Nine Dash Line. China has built up the atolls and islands within the Nine Dash Line and equipped them with military bases, airports for jet fighters, and land-to-sea and land-to-air missiles. The territory of the Nine Dash Line is thus now heavily fortified and armed by China.

CHAPTER 3

Joint maneuvers with Russia in that area underline that neither country wants the USA and the West to exercise its traditional dominance in the region.

China gains from these maneuvers. China, now with the world's largest navy, does not need the Russian navy in the South China Sea except as an additional source of intimidation for the West. Russia gains little from its own Pacific reach, except for the inference of friendship between the two countries, which creates a larger group of countries challenging the United States.

Russia is not primarily a nation of export manufactures, but it works with China on up-to-date armaments and on interchangeability of weaponry. The principal economic cooperation is Russia as a supplier of natural gas to China, which is chronically short of gas. The Power of Siberia pipeline was built between the countries, started shipping gas in 2019 from Russia to China, and will be up to full capacity in 2025. There is therefore a degree of interdependence between the two countries, a source of needed gas for China and a source of income for Russia.

Russia never forgets that China with its 1.4 billion people is located on the soft, thinly populated underbelly of Russia, rich in undeveloped resources and, at least in concept, a region that could be imagined from a Chinese viewpoint as expansion space for China. That will not happen in the near future as long as the "marriage of convenience" provides worthwhile benefits and Russia stays strong. With a change of heart within China and consciousness that expansion space is needed, this could again become a threat to Russia.

Occasional conflicts between the two are inevitable, especially in central Asia, as was illustrated in Kazakhstan this year, where Russia dispatched its military at the request of Kazakh leadership and China could only stand by and watch, a demonstration of China's lack of reach at a critical time into a "belt and road" country. It was a low-key, little publicized loss of face for China, something China never likes.

The principal focus of the relationship is a shared rivalry with, and dislike of, past USA hegemony, and for China, a distraction from its own aggressive activities inside the Nine Dash Line and Southeast Asia that Russia can offer through its imperial ambitions in Ukraine and in eastern Europe.

Aggressive activities of Russia in central Asia and eastern Europe can create an opportunity by distracting Western attention if China decides that the moment is right to reunite Taiwan with the mainland by force. Simultaneous aggression by Russia on one front and aggression by China in Asia will be hard for the West to handle.

Xi and Putin watch the United States repeatedly and endlessly harming itself through internal divisions. They are likely to say to each other, "the United States is declining as a threat to our ambitions; we don't have to face the United States frontally, the United States is tearing itself apart without effort on our part."

Self-destructive, self-indulgent behavior as we are undergoing in the United States would never be permitted in China or in Russia.

As recently as February 2022, at the Beijing Winter Olympics, Putin and Xi met together and issued a statement saying that the two countries were now extremely close, with Xi calling Putin, "my best friend."

In February it looked as if Putin would do more of the posturing that was so successful for him with the invasion of Georgia in 2008 and the seizure of Crimea in 2014, neither of which resulted in consequences for Russia or for Putin. He got away with both actions because the West, especially Europe, wanted to believe that Putin would stop with threats and not move to actual military invasion.

Both Putin and Xi must take wary account of the United States, suffering from self-inflicted social wounds, and may reflect that the United States is less of an issue and an obstacle and hope that, left to its own devices, the United States will decline further. Happily for Putin and Xi, the United States has become its own worst enemy.

The world wanted to believe in January and February 2022 that Putin's stationing of 125,000 troops and military attack equipment on the borders of Ukraine was merely posturing, another Putin threat that would be reduced through diplomacy. However this time it was different: right on the heels of promises to the French president and the German chancellor and to the USA that Russia would not invade, Putin did invade.

CHAPTER 3

That was a disappointment for Emmanuel Macron, who tried to see the good side of Putin and repeatedly encouraged conversation between Russia, France, and the West.

The invasion had a result different from what Putin expected. The Ukrainians resisted vigorously and with early success in the hilly terrain north of Kiev. Not only were severe sanctions imposed on Russia, likely to harm the Russian economy, but Germany closed down work on the second line of the Nord Stream gas pipeline and increased its military spending to 2 percent of its GNP.

Germany's decades-long accommodating posture to Russia was reversed in a matter of days by a social democrat government, which in the past was positioned towards accommodation with Russia.

Worse from Putin's standpoint, the tepid relationship between Europe and the United States was revived, with both Europe and the United Kingdom all stating strong support for NATO. Both Russia and China were surprised at the extent and depth of reach-out by the United States to traditional allies following the Russian invasion of Ukraine. It was quite a wake-up call for Putin, and at a distance, for Xi.

In this situation China, which had Ukraine as a client state for investments and loans and which is located on the Belt and Road initiative to which China is deeply committed, and in light of China's policy of honoring borders, the Russian attack on Ukraine weeks after the declaration of "best friend" was an uncomfortable and embarrassing event.

If Putin did not tell Xi that he was actually going to invade Ukraine, he concealed the truth, putting Xi into a difficult situation. Following on the statement of "best friends," what Putin may have done to Xi is worse than lying about his intention to invade, as Putin did to Macron, Scholz, and Biden. "Best friends" do not conceal matters of critical importance from each other.

China defends itself on the issue of Ukraine by saying that it sympathizes with the threat to its security that Russia feels from NATO and that the idea of Ukraine joining NATO is anathema.

CHAPTER 3

China sees a comparable threat to its security in the growing defense consultations among the United States, Australia, Japan, and India, while China conveniently ignores its own occupation and quietly executed militarization of islands and atolls inside the Nine Dash Line in the South China Sea. That seems to have had no political cost or bad consequences for China.

China wants to have things its way but does not want to risk joining Russia in being seen as aggressor in Ukraine; China is so closely, so extensively, involved in world trade on which it depends that it will seek to quietly distance itself from Putin for the present, which may not be a very long present.

In the past six months, Xi and Putin have learned something from each other. Putin has learned from Xi that eliminating political competition, even strong supporters in an autocratic country like Russia, can be important to political stability. Putin has started arresting and jailing persons like Dmitry Kolker and Vladimir Mau, both of whom favor a more open Russian society. In arresting such persons, Putin is taking a leaf from Xi's book. A number of leading Russians who had misgivings about the war in Ukraine have died in mysterious circumstances since February 24, 2022.

Xi, in turn, is watching Putin with care and, I imagine, admiration, as Putin plays a weak economic hand and possibly weak military hand against the West to secure his aggression in Ukraine and gradually taking control, to Russia's benefit, of the most valuable part of Ukraine's economy, that in the east.

What Putin is learning from Xi is to secure his sole position in charge by eliminating rivals in a time of contradictions, and what Xi is learning from Putin is how to get away with aggression against another country, a lesson that could be useful later.

The reintegration of Taiwan into China may be off the table for only a very brief period. At the moment, China wants to be seen as an understanding friend of Russia yet a responsible citizen of the world. This benign period may not last.

That the relationship between China and Russia is a marriage of convenience and not a marriage of love is an opportunity for the United States. This will be the subject of Part VI of this book.

CHAPTER 4

The not-so-minor players in the league of potential contenders – North Korea

As in the case of Russia, China, and the United States, history is the parent of present-day realities. Korea has a history going far back into neolithic times and an advanced civilization for thousands of years, a distinctive people, language, literature, culture, and customs that have resisted the incursions and, from time to time, the rule by powerful outsiders China and Japan. Part of the Korean story is the ability to survive between these two powerful, and normally opposed, cultures and remain their own way, as a highly significant contributor to the culture and history and evolution of mankind.

Korea was occupied by Japan and actually annexed by Japan from 1910 to 1945, a most unsatisfactory time for Korea as Japanese occupiers did their utmost to extinguish Korean culture, language, and customs and Koreans were often forced to "japanify" their names. During World War II Korean women served as "comfort women" to the Japanese army, and Korean men were impressed into it.

With the defeat of Japan in World War II Korea was liberated in the south by Americans and in the north by Soviet Russia and China. That stark difference led to the Korean war in June 1950 and, later, to the establishment of two separate countries: Democratic People's Republic of Korea, north of the 38th parallel, and the Republic of Korea, south of the 38th Parallel.

North Korea became an autocracy, the most severe and forbidding anywhere in the world, ruled by the Kim family, now in its third generation of absolute rule. South Korea became a functioning democracy, with at times very hard and corrupt presidents and ruling parties. South Korea has been a very open country, increasingly a world trade and technology leader, that greatly benefited from the markets of the West. North Korea is known as the "hermit kingdom," severely restrictive for its citizens.

Bottom line on their relative success: South Korea has a population of 52 million people, North Korea has a population of 26 million people, the economy of South Korea is fifty-four times the size of the economy of North Korea, reflecting completely different ways of rule and economy. North Korea is a country of privilege for the very few at the top, South Korea is a democracy that enjoys prosperity for most everyone.

North Korea is the world's bad boy: shut off from the rest of the world except China by its own choice and own policies, it lives a life of the underworld. With a very low standard of living its principal need for foreign earnings is to support the Kim regime in power and to develop its military power. North Korea developed nuclear weapons with help from Abdul Qadeer Khan of Pakistan, who developed his own country's atomic weapons. Khan then set about proliferating nuclear weapons, at a price, to all comers.

For its illegal activities in drugs and nuclear weaponry and missile tests North Korea has been heavily sanctioned. Its policy can be best described like this: with no relative power in the world of trade, there is little possibility for the manufacture and exchange of goods to better the lives of its citizens. North Korea is on a search to get the world's attention, like a bad child that throws tantrums.

With the exception of Donald Trump, no other world leader has paid personal attention to North Korea, and the overtures of South Korea have been substantially ignored by the North. The aim of North Korea is to retain its system and be respected and slightly feared by the United States, just as a bad child would hope.

Vladimir Putin has lately given a helping hand to North Korea by importing North Korean labor to occupied zones in eastern Ukraine, a source of income to North Korea and a source of relatively cheap labor for Russia at a time when people willing to work in dangerous zones are scarce.

What is interesting, and China surely thinks about it too, is that despite the seeming long-standing friendship between the nations, North Korea's missiles and nuclear weapons are closer to China than to any other country except South Korea, which may give China some uncomfortable, very private, afterthoughts. The combination of nuclear weapons and long-range missiles gives rise to dangerous hubris.

CHAPTER 4

The problem of North Korea is not easy to solve. It may end in a misadventure, a nuclear-loaded missile sent off accidentally by the North, intercepted, and immediate and devastating reprisals resulting in the collapse of the regime and of course death and injury for millions in North Korea and in the vicinity in China and South Korea.

Much better would be a gradual dialogue that could detoxify North Korea, bring it into the family of nations, relaxing the Kim family rule but leaving the Kim family in charge. This would have been a job for an extraordinary diplomat like the late Chou En-lai of China, but there is no one on the political global landscape of a stature able to take this on.

Iran

I worked frequently in Iran during the time of the Shah, before 1979, and came to know Iran well. It was clear to me already in the 1960s that Iran had the potential to be a very great country and that the Persian people were gifted and resourceful and hardworking. I thought of Iran as "the Japan of the Middle East" and that it would be a major mistake to ever underestimate Iran or the potential of its people. Nothing has changed in my view of that country and its people.

Iran has a long and highly cultivated history, rich in art and literature and highly skilled at international relations. The people of Iran, the Persians, known in ancient times as the Parthians, are among the ancient civilizations of the world that managed to survive despite the power of the Moguls of India on the south, Russia on its northern border, and in ancient times Greece. It is an interesting parallel to Korea in that Iran has had cultural influences outside the borders that have attempted to control the country.

Russia may look like a friend to Iran now, but that was anything but true during World War II when Soviet Russia and Britain together attacked Iran. The Soviet Union occupied the northern half of the country, including Tehran, and only left in 1946.

Like Korea, Iran has extraordinary expertise at survival. A story that illustrates Persia's remarkable diplomatic skills relates to a gold and emerald box held among Iran's national treasures in the vault of Bank Melli Iran in Tehran. The box is unique because of the size of the emeralds: each side and the top and bottom of the box, which is probably five inches long, is a single emerald, a piece of jewelry unparalleled anywhere. As the story goes, the emerald box was in the turban of an Indian mogul that Persia had recently defeated in battle. The then Shah of Persia and the Mogul were together discussing peace; the Shah had heard that the box was concealed in the Mogul's turban and he said, "In Persia when we want friendship with a nation, our leaders exchange hats" It was impossible for the Mogul to object, hats were exchanged, and Persia thus acquired this unique jeweled box.

Iran's diplomatic skills are now at work in the renegotiation of the 2015 agreement against Iran developing a nuclear bomb, an agreement that President Trump pulled out of because he thought it inadequate. In place of that, there is nothing, and Iran has neatly "exchanged hats" with the West in general and the United States in particular.

Underpinning the Iran regime is that it is by far the largest Shiite Muslim country. The Shia Muslims have been historically at odds with the far more numerous Sunni Muslims since the death of the Prophet Mohammad in 632 AD. At the time of the death of Mohammad part of the community chose to back Ali, son-in-law and cousin of the Prophet, becoming the Shia, rather than Abu Baker, who was backed by the majority, which became the Sunni. The historical dislike of nearly 1,400 years between the Sunni and the Shia will never go away.

A curious aspect is that during the 1960s and 1970s Iran and Israel were on excellent terms, right over the heads of the Arab nations that lay geographically between them. Trade flourished, there was investment, all of which, seemingly, stopped after the takeover in 1979 by Abdullah Ruhollah Khomeini and the Muslim Mullahs. Even as late as the 1990s, long after the regime of the Mullahs had taken power, there were reliable reports that Iran was acquiring military hardware from Israel, proof once again that appearances are often different from reality. Outward declarations of hatred may be cover for highly productive secret relations.

Through the United States invasion of Iraq in 2003 we made a gift to Iran of Iraq, which was ruled by minority Sunni people, as Shiites are now the dominant influence in Iraq. To the surprise of Iran, the strongest Shia religious and political faction in Iraq has started resisting Iranian involvement in running Iraq.

Do we even in the United States understand these things that we have done in 2003, or care? They are critical to the people involved, and knowledge and understanding of them is extremely important to the United States – whether we like it or not.

Iran after the fall of the Shah in 1979 has a clerical regime of Mullahs allegedly fired by religion but in reality a "strongman" regime, now led by cleric Ali Khamenei. The objective of the regime is to remain in power, and like other autocratic regimes, privilege and serious wealth and lavish living is reserved for the people in charge at the top.

Having all privileges and being in full control, why would the Mullahs want to relinquish any of the benefits? A very strong, well-armed military enjoys popular support and backs the regime of Mullahs. There are elections in Iran, but the real power is in the hands of the Iranian military and the top clerics. Outsiders do not have access to or information about this inner circle.

Unlike North Korea, despite sanctions in place the Iranian economy has managed to survive; there are millions of poor people in the countryside, but in the cities there is a growing, relatively prosperous, and well-informed middle class with family members abroad, aspirations, and a good standard of living. Unlike North Koreans, Iranians can leave the country if they wish and can travel, though Iran remains a repressive police state for its opponents.

Iran has developed its international power through its skilled creation and management of proxy forces such as Shiite cliques in Iraq, paramilitary forces in Syria, the Houthi in Yemen, and Hezbollah in Lebanon. These forces have been effective in projecting Iranian power and damaging their adversaries. As they project Iranian power they do much disruption and much harm, at the base of which is the Sunni–Shia rivalry.

That Iran has supplied "kamikaze" drones in quantity to Russia, which Russia in turn uses against military targets and the civilian population in Ukraine, is a source of income for Iran but does not improve Iran's image in the community of nations.

CHAPTER 4

The situation of Iran is vastly better and simpler, potentially, than that of North Korea. The strongmen, the clericals and the military, on top in Iran want to keep their system for their personal benefit but they are pragmatic in having the Iranian people enjoy an improving standard of living and a secure future, provided there is an acceptable level of obedience to religious rules.

Despite repression, the clerics have skillfully developed Iranian nationalism, which supports the military and backs adventures of their proxies, a big part of Iran's overseas influence. The Iranian military seeks to build on its influence, and that is a risk to the region and to the world. If Iran completes building a nuclear bomb and announces it, it will likely lead to a regional arms race and more hostilities.

Iranians have the talent and the energy, the culture and the history, to be a contributor to the world and the populace, not the leadership, wants to be in and of the world.

Iran is both an opportunity and a threat. Iran should stop its attacks on other nations through proxies. If that can be done, and firmly adhered to, Iran needs to be brought back into the family of nations. Iran and the West need to come to terms, make an agreement that is mutually beneficial, ensures peace, lowers barriers, and returns money and prisoners, and gradually establish trust. That will be of benefit to humanity, to stability and prosperity in Iran and throughout the human family. At the moment, preventing Iran from building nuclear weapons and bringing Iran into the community of nations are both extremely difficult and unlikely, a double tragedy.

CHAPTER 5

Other key countries
How each fits into the Russia-China-USA mosaic

Following the Russian attack on Ukraine, the April 7, 2022, United Nations resolution to suspend Russia from the Human Rights Council received ninety-three countries voting in favor, twenty-four countries against, and very interestingly, fifty-eight abstentions. The abstentions included India, Indonesia, Brazil, South Africa, and Mexico. The reasoning of each country is different, but there is a point in common, an underpinning to the abstentions: the decline in credibility and global influence of the United States during the past twenty years.

Turkey

Turkey voted "yes" on the resolution to suspend Russia from the Human Rights Council, and as we read the news, Turkey is more of a political enigma than many other countries, but the issues are not as complicated as they seem. Turkey has all along been an important member of NATO. Its size and its unique location controlling both sides of the Bosporus give it the ability and the power to control access to the Black Sea, who goes in and who comes out. Countries that depend on Turkey's consent for access to and from the Black Sea include Russia, Ukraine, and Georgia, as well as EU members Romania and Bulgaria.

Turkey appears to have drifted away from the West; the fundamental reasons for this are two.

One, Turkey wants to be considered as a European country and made its original application to the EEC in 1987; it became eligible to be a candidate for membership in the European Union in 1999. Since then the application has not materially advanced and in June this year the European Parliament let Turkey know that it has to make internal political changes before its membership can advance. What Turkey sees as foot-dragging by the European Union has not been appreciated by the Erdogan government, which has taken an increasingly Islamist turn, different from the model that Kemal Ataturk, the founder of the republic of modern Turkey, created in 1923.

Erdogan is strongly against Kurdish efforts to create an autonomous state in Turkey, yet Kurds in northern Syria have fought effectively against Al Qaeda, thus enjoying support from the United States.

Two, the reduced American presence in the Middle East that started during the Obama administration has greatly reduced American influence in the region. The fact that Erdogan's Turkey is a member of NATO but holds meetings with Putin and Iran after the invasion of Ukraine and is increasing its trade with Russia at a time when Russia is under sanctions shows that Turkey is keeping its options open, a very unsettling factor in an unstable yet crucial part of the world.

Turkey has serious economic problems in its sky-high inflation and depreciation in the value of its currency. What happens in Turkey is strongly driven by the politics of Erdogan and present high inflation and decline in value of the currency. Turkey is not so much undecided as it is playing both sides, something it can afford to do because of its position controlling access to the Black Sea. No one can ignore Turkey or minimize its importance.

India

India with its population of 1.4 billion is so large that it is by its very size a major player. India was among the abstainers from the April 7 resolution out of concern about offending Russia, a longtime supplier of armaments to India, considered as an ally, not so far as to join in war together but a political supporter.

Conversely, India has major issues with China, on the mountainous border between the countries where there has been sporadic fighting, and in the Indian Ocean, and in Sri Lanka, where China has made economic and military inroads. India does not want to offend Russia and views the China-Russia alliance with concern, so India does not go out of its way to offend China. Yet India is joining Japan, the USA, and Australia in a loose arrangement to defend free maritime passage in the South China Sea.

That however is not all: India is joining Russia, China, and Belarus in military exercises together, something it has done in the past. India has since its establishment as an independent country in 1947 worked in the middle of the road, friendly with Russia while always seeking to be on the good side of the United States.

India is a giant to be reckoned with, and it can do what it wants. It is accustomed since many decades to border skirmishes with China, and while very irritating and an internal political issue, it has learned to live with them. A new era may be starting for India in naval competition with China in the Indian Ocean, which may move India to becoming closer to the West.

Israel

Israel is a country that has greatly changed in recent years. It has become a significant designer and manufacturer of technological software, including for supervision of populations and for weaponry, with growing, largely under the radar screen, demand for its software products.

Concurrently Israel, starting under the Trump administration with the Abraham Accords, has made great strides in relationships with Arab countries. In addition to its relationships with Egypt and Jordan, Israel has full diplomatic ties with Qatar and the United Arab Emirates.

It also has the right to overfly Saudi Arabia and likely, a secret, off-the-record and likely very effective relationship with Saudi Arabia in regard to the most pressing problem that the two countries jointly share, containment of Iran.

The evolution of Israel during recent years is, for a person like me, very familiar with the Middle East and its politics, the most dramatic change in the region, even more so than the change in power in Egypt, Tunisia, and the civil war in Syria.

Israel has become not only respectable but important and useful to many Arab countries, resulting in a degree of regional boredom with the seventy-five-year-old issue of the seizure of Arab lands and displacement of Palestinians.

The world has changed, interests are different, and the biggest supporter of the Palestinians is Iran, which uses the issue not so much to benefit the Palestinians but as a lever against Sunni Arab countries.

CHAPTER 5

The people who suffer from this continuing mess are the Palestinians themselves, those who have not been fortunate enough to extricate themselves from refugee camps and secure passports from surrounding Arab countries and work permits. Very few Palestinians have been able to do this, and those in camps, for example in Lebanon, have no rights or privileges and are kept, by tradition, with the support of the United Nations, as pawns in the long-standing effort to threaten Israel.

In reality the world has moved on. Many formerly committed watchers have lost interest, and Iran is now the only player that still uses the Palestinians as a proxy weapon.

Saudi Arabia

Saudi Arabia has greatly changed in recent years under the de facto rule of Crown Prince Mohammed bin Salman, son of elderly King Salman. As a person who has known Saudi Arabia well since 1967, I am among its defenders: understanding how well informed the Saudi leadership has been in world affairs. Over the years, things have greatly changed for the better: the influence of radicalizing religious schools is a potential threat to the state and has been greatly reduced.

In some cases the Mullahs in charge of such schools have been arrested and tried for harming the state; women are at work, women and men mix socially, women drive cars and travel without a male escort and Prince Salman has a long-term plan to make Saudi Arabia a technology leader and reduce dependence on its wealth of fossil fuels.

If you travel to Saudi Arabia now, there are both female and male immigration officers. Some readers who are critical of Saudi Arabia may find this unremarkable, but for me it represents light-years of progress. Travel yourself to Saudi Arabia, meet young people, and you will feel the optimism in the air.

When I was there in 2019 a company that I know well had their young employees, men and women, design a gold pin to give out at an international convention being held in Riyadh. The pin is attractive, round, gold plated, and stunning: on the pin are the arms of Saudi Arabia and the words "A Solid Nation" in English.

CHAPTER 5

The impression I had was that this was how young Saudi men and women feel about their country. It had me reflecting, how many young American men and women would describe the United States as "a solid nation"?

Saudi Arabia and the United States have been friends since King AbdelAziz and President Franklin Roosevelt met seventy-seven years ago in February 1945 on board the cruiser USS Quincy.

I had the remarkable experience of meeting then King Feisal in 1967, who said, "when I'm in the United States I am among friends."

The relationship with Saudi Arabia has been seriously and unnecessarily neglected. Today we think of the relationship as being not only in disrepair, but declining further.

Decline of United States presence in the Middle East has been a factor. A larger contribution has been reluctance to see the benefits to the Saudi people that Crown Prince Mohammed bin Salman has brought and to view them with a supportive eye.

Poland, Lithuania, Latvia, and Estonia

Poland and the Baltics, along with Moldova, Romania, and Bulgaria, are the countries with the most to lose if Russia wins in Ukraine, regroups, and considers what next of the former Russian/Soviet empire it should attack and recover. Poland and the Baltics have been raising the alarm in the EU, galvanizing western Europeans for whom they provide a geographical cushion against Belarus and Russia.

From the start of the Ukraine war, Poland has been exemplary, receiving over a million refugees from Ukraine, helping refugees find places to live, giving them the right to work, putting children in school, the most generous treatment of refugees in history. As the expression goes, "they know whereof they speak." Eastern Europe has lived through it all: Soviet occupation, lack of opportunity, lack of a vigorous economy. They don't want it again. But now they are members of NATO, and under the NATO treaty, an attack on one country must be defended by all.

CHAPTER 5

Finland and Sweden

The membership of NATO will soon, if Turkey gives its consent, be increased by Finland, with its army of 300,000 soldiers, and Sweden, in both cases a very big plus in defending Europe.

Finland has had bitter experience in defending itself against the Soviet Union in 1940; since then it has had deep suspicion, alert to threats, and has remained heavily armed.

Sweden has internal issues that are a major preoccupation: uncontrolled refugee immigration, and law and order. The Swedish government is accused of having left personal security to chance because of alleged leftist sympathies, and indeed, crime and murder have hugely increased in a country which was formerly safe. The Swedish election held on September 11 holds the possibility of future change.

Western Europe and the United Kingdom

The history of Europe is one of virtually constant wars in large part among the countries that are today members of the peaceful European Union. The Hundred Years War, the Thirty Years War, the Franco-Prussian war, World War I, and World War II were major ones, with many lesser ones as European countries fought each other abroad, including in the American Revolutionary War.

When it comes to war, Europe has experienced it forever and war remains part of Europe's consciousness.

The strong desire to avoid war and lead a peaceful life, and lifestyle, that Europe enjoys led to wishful thinking on the part of European nations and a truly startling wake-up call on February 24, 2022, when Russia invaded Ukraine. The wake-up call was amplified by assurances by Vladimir Putin to both Olaf Scholz of Germany and Emmanuel Macron of France that Russia would not invade Ukraine despite a large Russian army being massed on Ukraine's borders.

Putin lied, and that suddenly became part of the new European consciousness.

France, Germany, the United Kingdom, Mario Draghi's Italy, and Switzerland have all been steadfast about supporting Ukraine, despite the great worries they have and share about the availability of natural gas especially as the seasons move into autumn and winter. France has supplied weapons to Ukraine, the United Kingdom has provided weapons and training, Germany has promised weapons but is still hoping the nightmare of cutoff from Russian gas will go away.

It will not.

Not least, it has emerged that Russia has no problem at all in selling its gas to China, to India, and Russia is receiving plenty of cash, which has bolstered its economy. One buyer, Europe, that was dependent on the gas, was replaced by others happy to buy it.

The United Kingdom deserves further detail because it is unique among European countries to have joined as a member of the European Union and subsequently left it. That departure is known as Brexit. Fortunately for Ukraine the departure of the United Kingdom from the European Union has not affected Britain's strong support for Ukraine in having been invaded by Russia.

The United Kingdom is a special case, in light of the stunning "own goal" it made when it withdrew from the European Union. That the United Kingdom painted itself into a corner is not much spoken of, but real nonetheless. In withdrawing from the European Union the United Kingdom cut off easy access to a European market of 250 million people, which gave Britain critical market mass of which it was a part.

Less well understood, Britain's quitting membership of the European Union deprived prospective investors in European manufacturing of an enormous asset: the English language, certainly a factor in the decisions years ago of Japanese companies to set up manufacturing businesses aimed at the entire European market.

Next it deprived Britain of easy movement of labor from other parts of the Union to the United Kingdom, a force in attracting more flexible talent and lowering costs as well as an influx of young Europeans to set up businesses in the United Kingdom. That effect has made Ashford, Kent, virtually a French city, an advantage all around and great for the British economy.

CHAPTER 5

Further, the departure of Britain from the European Union has greatly slowed down integration of the British and Irish economies and, if that were not enough, threatens a political problem on the borders among Northern Ireland, which is part of the United Kingdom, and Ireland because of customs border practices to which the United Kingdom agreed in its Brexit departure treaty from Europe. Finally, Scotland wanted to remain in the European Union, and the fact that it did not gave Scottish leader Nicola Sturgeon a lever against the United Kingdom in event of a future Scottish referendum.

This unnecessary mess happened because of two things: David Cameron, then British prime minister, did not focus on the referendum issue in 2016 and make the "remain" (i.e., stay in the European Union) case seriously enough to ensure massive passage. Also many English voters, especially older people, at the time of the referendum in 2016 "voted with their hearts instead of with their heads."

Following the departure of Boris Johnson as Prime Minister in 2022, the then new prime minister Liz Truss, an able person was herself a "remainer" at the time of the 2016 referendum. Truss announced economic steps that scared financial markets; she then reversed her own decisions. Faced with massive instability and loss of confidence her government lasted only 44 days. The incoming Prime Minister is Rishi Sunak, previously Chancellor of the Exchequer under Boris Johnson. The outlook for stability under Rishi Sunak is reasonable, bearing in mind that tough decisions have to be made about inflation, expenditure and the people's living standards. He will need luck on his side.

The underlying *leitmotiv* of every economic problem in the United Kingdom is Brexit. Britain is stuck with it, the market of the European Union will never be replaced, although the chances for the United Kingdom are better if China and the United States follow the recommendation for permanent friendship in this book. There is no practical way to return to the reality and mentality of "little England."

CHAPTER 5

Japan

The transition from a military empire in 1945 to a true functioning democracy with the emperor as figurehead, all accomplished bloodlessly under a military occupation, is one of the remarkable political events of all time.

Never underestimate Japan.

Despite the aging of its population and economic stagnation for several decades, Japan offers a good living to its population, relative equality of economic classes compared to many countries, and a source of highly creative technology.

Pacifism is a part of its constitution, and the limited Japanese military is clearly denominated as self-defense forces. That said, a result of the great tsunami of 2011, with many lives lost and towns destroyed and damage to nuclear power plants, was to underline Japan's dependence on imported oil and the shipping lanes from the Middle East.

China's claim to the Senkaku islands, which Japan claims as its own and China calls the Diao Yu, irritated by Chinese naval vessels in the surrounding Japanese waters, has created a gradual change of mindset from the taking peace for granted. Likewise Japan is very concerned about China's threats to Taiwan, more so even than other neighboring countries in Southeast Asia.

Japan has been host to American military bases since the end of World War II, and the United States is, by treaty, the guarantor of Japan's security. The lack of clear policy definition during the Obama administration, the pullback from engagement during the Trump administration, and the wavering and chaos in Afghanistan under the Biden administration all have contributed to concern about American steadfastness.

Under late Prime Minister Shinzo Abe there was new interest in increased militarization to create stronger defense. Japan is quietly rumored to have the technology to make nuclear weapons as well as hypersonic missiles, which China has, North Korea claims to have, and the United States is now working on.

CHAPTER 5

Japan has joined with the United States, the United Kingdom, and Australia in a mutual defense pact, AUKUS, in the Pacific, deeply unsettling to China.

Australia

After a long honeymoon with China, Australia is having a wake-up call. As the principal supplier of iron ore to a growing Chinese economy, Australia had a large dependable income from exports of commodities that seemed as if it would go on forever. The Chinese language became part of Australian school curricula, just as Japanese had been in Australian schools a generation earlier.

Then China in 2021 placed an embargo on Australian wine imports as punishment for Australia's criticism of China. Concurrently, Australia took note of Chinese growing relationships in the Pacific north of Australia, in Papua, in Kiribati, in the Solomon Islands. Distant Australia started feeling threatened by Chinese submarine capabilities.

In 2021 Australia terminated a project for French designed and made submarines, opting instead to join with the United Kingdom and the United States in designing and manufacturing a new, advanced class of nuclear submarines for joint cooperation and defense in the Pacific.

Australia is feeling very uneasy about China. Like Japan, it is doing something about it.

Republic of Korea

One of the great technology and manufacturing centers of the world, South Korea did it all on its own, aided by the demand for broad-based consumer technology and access to the American market, combined with the presence of a major contingent of US forces based in Korea to defend the country together with their own formidable, very able forces. The size and success of the South Korean economy stands in dramatic contrast to the poverty, oppression, and low standard of living in North Korea, which however is nuclear armed and the source of unremitting threats against the South.

South Korea has to play carefully for fear of offending China, its largest single customer for semiconductors and other consumer goods. It is not a part of the defense pact that includes Japan, in part only because of strained relations with Japan dating back to World War II, but that does not obscure its vital interest in keeping the international waters in the South China Sea open to its shipping, including imports of oil.

South Korea and Japan have concerns that are similar between the two countries, worrisome ones that they do not appear to openly discuss with each other. A connecting tie between the countries is the United States and its military bases.

Both countries hope that the United States is dependable in its undertaking to protect them.

Emerging markets – Africa and Latin America

Quietly, China and Russia as well have made great economic inroads in Africa and in Latin America. In some cases Chinese support has worked out, in other cases not.

I don't blame China, but I do blame us in the United States for being asleep at the switch while this was happening over at least three decades. We failed to pay attention to these regions and countries and took for granted that we Americans did not have to make a significant effort in supporting their economic development.

Because of economic ties on commodities, major projects financed with loans from China and barely visible political ties, many African and Latin American countries have not wanted to offend Russia and its ally China, hence are among the countries that voted against suspending Russia from the Human Rights Council or abstained from the vote condemning Russia for its invasion of Ukraine.

A further aspect comes into it with some of the African countries that feel slighted when Europe and the West give insufficient attention to aggressions by one country against another on the African continent. Having been left alone to deal with African issues themselves, like the bloody local war between Tutsis and Hutus in Rwanda, without much outside concern, there is a latent sense of satisfaction when one European country attacks another, a shrug of the shoulders, that the invasion of Ukraine is a problem for Europeans. "Neglect us here, and we shall turn our backs on you there."

African abstention on these issues speaks as loudly as a "no."

The situation in Latin America is more politically polarized. While Cuba was alone in having Russian and Chinese backing decades ago, that is not true today. Venezuela, Bolivia, Nicaragua, El Salvador, and Argentina have left-leaning governments with some degree of Chinese and Russian backing, a chance for those sponsor countries to weaken US influence in Latin America, at very little cost, in large part the result of American neglect of the region.

Diffidence about Russia's invasion of Ukraine is a symbol paying the price at the United Nations for American neglect of Africa and Latin America.

Part II
The United States

CHAPTER 6

Historical background 1776 to 1945
– geography and immigration

The independence of the United States in 1776 was an example and a beacon to people around the world, and despite some diminution, remains so today. A large share of American colonials did not want to be ruled from England in the eighteenth century, and with the help of England's rival France, the United States threw off the colonial yoke in the Revolutionary War, achieved freedom from England, and became its own nation.

Freedom is the key. "Life, liberty and the pursuit of happiness" are enshrined in the US Declaration of Independence, and they are basic to American thinking, "inalienable" rights, ones that cannot be put aside. Americans feel that their destiny and freedom are their own, as individuals and as a country, and that no one can take these away.

An influence in the makeup of our thinking is our geography, with the Atlantic Ocean on the right and the Pacific Ocean on the left, we were historically far distanced from other powers by water, especially from the ongoing destructive rivalries among powers in Europe, and we benefited from having friendly countries to the north and the south.

Canada, a dominion of the British Commonwealth, is dedicated to independence and to charting its own future, albeit with a residue of affection for the mother country, England, not so strong that it prevented removal of the British ensign from the national flag and its replacement by the Canadian maple leaf in 1965.

Mexico does not share the history and traditions of the United States. In cultural and historical ways its history was strongly opposed, but the two countries are tied together economically and geographically and interests are for the most part mutually beneficial. That Canada and Mexico are on American borders are tremendous advantages for the United States and indeed for Canada and Mexico. Sore points are the drug trade, some of which transits

Mexico, and the stream of refugees coming into the United States, to which our own absence of firm policy and control greatly contributes.

The advantageous geography of the United States vis-à-vis Europe and Asia diminished in importance over time with the advent of long-distance aviation, intercontinental ballistic missiles, more countries having nuclear weapons, and far more rapidly though less obviously with the endless applications of the Internet, including for cyber-warfare.

The mentality inside the United States has changed less than the surrounding global reality. There is an feeling among Americans that the United States is a large country, large in capabilities and large in territory, with a long-running record of success in whatever tasks had to be undertaken. We take for granted and do not question that we are masters of our own destiny. We have fought wars that defeated the enemies of the United States and its allies, and we have been of irreplaceable value to other countries in retaining their territory and their freedom, notably in the First and Second World Wars.

A remarkable fact, in which we should take pride, is that despite all our internal divisions the United States is still today the destination of choice for immigrants from all over the world, if only it is possible. What is it that makes the United States a preferred choice compared to beacons of freedom like Britain, France, Germany, Canada, Australia, and New Zealand?

Two aspects are important: first, the United States remains a seemingly unstructured society, less so in appearance than in reality. Newcomers and their families feel that it's possible to be "absorbed" into American society and find one's own place more easily in a country where nearly everyone's antecedents were immigrants than in countries with a highly defined and admired historical culture.

Second, the United States is a society more forgiving of failure. If a newcomer fails at something and has not become a criminal with a record, there may be a different path open later to the resourceful and hardworking immigrant. Early failure, short of a crime, is not readily remembered and not held against people in the United States, a society of short memories. If early failure is followed by success, it is success that is remembered until success becomes so overbearing that envy causes other people to dig into the past.

CHAPTER 6

An important perception of difference: immigrants fuel American society and the American economy, and the ongoing flow of persons arriving in the United States, mostly young working-age people often with young families, reenergizes the human capital of the country.

The influx of young immigrants reduces the problem of an aging society with a low birth rate so we in the United States escape a problem that Russia, most of Europe, and Japan have. China has the aging and lack of renewal problem too, in its case because of the special problem of the one-child family policy that turned out harmful to the future of the country.

Like the United States, our neighbor Canada has greatly benefited from relatively easy immigration that attracted large numbers of people from Asia and from the Middle East, contributing to what has become an increasingly dynamic Canadian society.

CHAPTER 7

From 1945 to 1950
The United States and Canada in prime time

In the immediate post–World War II year of 1945, the United States and Canada were unique among developed countries, because there had been no fighting on the home territory and therefore no destruction. American and Canadian industry had poured out a huge stream of aircraft, tanks, guns, and naval and merchant vessels that were a decisive element in winning World War II for the Allies, resources that the Axis powers Germany, Japan, and Italy did not have in comparable depth. There was widespread devastation from the war throughout Europe, the Soviet Union, Japan, and China as well as enormous loss of life.

After the war, US industry converted effectively and quickly to becoming the dominant global supplier of manufactured goods for the postwar period. The United States helped Europe to rebuild, and through its administration of Japan sought to help the economies and industries of Japan rebuild in a democracy, and the effort worked.

With time, hard work, and investment, in part by the United States, economies of other countries recovered. By the 1950s there was a German miracle and by the 1960s the Japanese miracle was in full force. Wherever American influence was felt, democracy flourished. Economic competition for United States industry grew in terms of both technology, cost, quality, and delivery. It was a by-product of the revival and growth of the world economy.

Large parts of the world became independent nations, mostly because the colonial powers of the past, England, France, Belgium, Italy, Portugal, the Netherlands, and Japan, did not have the human and financial resources to maintain colonial empires.

Italy lost its colonies in Africa during the war, England gave up India in 1947 and its African colonies over a number of years, the last big step being the exit from the British Empire of Southern Rhodesia to become Zimbabwe in 1980. Belgium gave up its enormous African colony Belgian Congo in 1960,

CHAPTER 7

Portugal gave up Angola and Mozambique in 1975, France was defeated by the Viet Cong in 1954 thus losing Indochina and gave up its African colonies and Algeria in 1962, the Netherlands lost the Dutch East Indies in 1949 after four years of fighting following the end of World War II.

The loss of colonies changed the mentality of these European former colonial powers, suffering early loss of wealth but later marshalling their enormous creative and productive power home and becoming far more successful economies themselves.

In planning their political future as independent nations, many young nations patterned themselves on the image of the United States as they perceived it. Australia and New Zealand were largely in the same situation as the United States but were not heavily industrialized. Because of the freedom and opportunity both offered, Australia and New Zealand and Canada likewise became role models for other, newer nations.

CHAPTER 8

The United States enters a competitive world – 1950 to 1975

From 1950 on things become more complicated.

For a number of reasons, change about the world seeped into our American cultural thinking gradually, difficult to perceive from year to year but easy to understand if comparing today in 2022 to the year 1945.

A realistic marker for change was the start of the Korean war in June 1950, a war in which the United States was deeply engaged. Unlike victory in World War I or World War II in which Americans played a decisive part, the Korean war ended in a stalemate in 1953 with Korea divided into two separate nations along the 38th Parallel, a line of demarcation set by the United States. North and South Korea are still formally at war which each other, sixty-nine years after the end of active military action against each other.

China and North Korea, backed by the Soviet Union, had held the United States, and its allies fighting for South Korea under the banner of the United Nations, to a draw, notwithstanding the enormous resources and lives committed to the conflict. The world took note of the less than satisfactory result of the war, the first nibbling away at the reality and image of the United States after the complete victory the United States and its allies achieved in World War II.

Two further political events were important in the perception of the United States by its own people and in the view of the United States from abroad. In 1959 the regime of Fulgencio Batista was overthrown and routed by a Communist group lead by a Cuban revolutionary, Fidel Castro, and a small group of people including Che Guevara, who became a romantic figure for aspiring revolutionaries throughout Latin America.

President John Kennedy was elected in 1960 and served as president until his assassination in November 1963 when he was succeeded by Lyndon Johnson.

CHAPTER 8

A US-backed attempt in 1961 to overthrow the Cuban regime was thwarted by Cuba in the Bay of Pigs, embarrassing for the United States. The presence of Russian intermediate-range, nuclear-armed missiles in Cuba, ninety miles from the continental United States, led to the Cuban missile crisis in 1962.

President Kennedy had to bargain with Nikita Khrushchev of the Soviet Union to reach an unequal agreement. Removing nuclear-armed missiles from Cuba under the agreement gave the Soviet Union a reward for its aggression in that American ICBMs were removed from Turkey. It was a chess game that ended in a draw.

The Communist regime established by Castro remains in power today, sixty-three years after its establishment, resulting in emigration of many of Cuba's able people and a life lacking in opportunity for those that remained. It was a loss of two generations of time for a highly talented people but gave privilege and power to Castro, his brother, and their successors and was an irritant to the United States, an unfriendly regime within ninety miles of the United States.

Important to understand is this: that in an autocratic regime like that of Cuba, and the Soviet Union, and Iran and North Korea and Venezuela today, those in charge, the small group at the top, benefit, but the people lose their freedom, the right and opportunity to make their lives, and that of their children, as they see fit. That is the real tragedy of North Korea, of what was formerly East Germany, of Myanmar and of every autocratic regime that requires its people to live the way the bosses on top say.

Little emphasized as such in the United States, the activity of Communist Cuba and Soviet Russia were violations of the Monroe Doctrine, enacted by President Monroe back in 1823. The rupture of the Monroe Doctrine created an example for other Latin America countries to become extreme left and autocratically ruled, including Nicaragua, Chile under Allende, and Venezuela.

Violation of the Monroe Doctrine became part of quietly accepted reality, the Doctrine sinking into the "dustbin of history," an expression coined by the Soviet dissident Leon Trotsky, a nibbling away at the American image and reality of influence.

CHAPTER 8

A major change in the United States and a source of serious division among Americans was the Vietnam war, which started in 1954 between France and the communist Vietminh. The United States had advisers to the government in South Vietnam as from the presidency of John F. Kennedy in 1961 and started active military involvement in 1965, withdrawing from the war after a secret agreement negotiated between US Secretary of State Henry Kissinger and North Vietnam in 1973.

The US military performed with valor and endurance in Vietnam in conditions that were extremely challenging. Rare among wars in which the United States was involved, the American population was divided as to whether the country should be in this war at all. Some of the persons drafted into the armed forces evaded the draft, some secured deferments on grounds of higher education, which created class differences, and the valorous and endangered military did not feel universally supported at home.

It was a time that gave the American people the experience of being divided over a major issue. Though about a war in Southeast Asia, division was an internal American issue. It was the first time since before World War II that Americans took opposing points of view on an issue that affected families and young people.

The experience of Vietnam legitimized self-examination and took the thrust away from building the nation, focused people on a matter that affected them deeply, highlighted differences of opinion, and chipped away at our global competitiveness.

Division would return to haunt the country in the twenty-first century.

Though the Vietnam war is rarely spoken of as a defeat for the United States, it was indeed a defeat, one in which a people remote from the United States, with a hard line Communist dictatorship in charge, forced us to negotiate and gave us a feeling of relief when that war was finally over.

The defeat of the United States in Vietnam entered into our deep consciousness, as something that really could happen, the acknowledgement of a weakness, of a required acceptance. Through the experience of Vietnam the United States was no longer invincible.

CHAPTER 8

Other than the Vietnam war the American standard of living continued well; middle-class family values predominated, losses of soldiers were an assault on the family. The sense that we were the greatest nation as from 1945 was only marginally touched.

The reality of our economic strength started to change around us. Aspiration to an economic middle-class lifestyle continued and was taken for granted. Jobs in industry remained plentiful in the USA and careers were often set for life, both in manufacturing and in service industries.

American industry was less responsive to American consumer preferences than growing competition from abroad. Manufacturers in foreign countries who exported to the United States produced goods that were different, sometimes more user-friendly, and had appeal of novelty.

US cars manufactured by GM, Ford, and Chrysler and American Motors in the 1960s and 1970s went through a period of poor quality in end products. Customers were unhappy, complained, but American manufacturers did not read "the handwriting on the wall," which gave an opening to British, German, and other European and Japanese manufacturers able to listen to and understand the wants of American customers. Sales of the Volkswagen "beetle" opened the US car market to competition on a substantial scale.

The same happened with refrigerators, air conditioners, vacuum cleaners, outboard motors, and at a later stage, trucks and industrial equipment. The USA became relatively less competitive in supplying its own home market; the changes happened slowly, hardly visible at the beginning.

CHAPTER 9

Developments abroad affecting the United States
The impact of technology

Education became an obsession in countries that were recovering from destruction from World War II. The period starting in the late 1940s started a boom in global education that continues today. Ancient universities were refreshed and expanded and new universities were started around the world, many dedicated to technological and scientific learning, and that boom in university organization and teaching spread all around the world to countries beyond western Europe and Japan.

By the mid-1970s there were large numbers of newly educated people in other countries, including developing countries. The United States and a handful of other countries no longer had a lock on higher education. Students learned in the United States and Europe and Asia and returned home with new skills.

The increase in people returning from universities abroad to home countries made technology transfer easier, as there were now educated people in the countries receiving technology as well as in those countries dispensing technology.

Outside the United States there was a tremendous growth of the middle class, people who increasingly had good jobs and wanted the benefits of their hard work in their lifestyle. In Europe people had refrigerators instead of ice boxes, comfortable apartments and homes, dependably warm in winter and cool on the hottest summer days, vacations away from home, good bathrooms, and motor cars.

American movies played a pivotal (and largely unappreciated) role in promoting a glamorous American lifestyle. In the movies, even blue-collar working Americans seemed to have a better life than Europeans. Vacations for middle-class Europeans changed from camping in a forest to getting on an airplane and traveling to Italy, to Spain, to the Balearic Islands.

In the 1960s and 1970s European compensation was usually lower than that in the United States, so that European manufacturers could compete successfully in the American market. That did not last. European labor was undersold by Japanese workers, and the miracle of industrial Japan was launched and flourished until the 1980s. People outside the United States worked hard, and worked smart, and as countries were undersold by cheaper labor from Japan or Southeast Asia they used technology to work their way up-market to higher-value goods.

Japan in turn was undersold by Southeast Asia and the opening of China through the visit of President Nixon and Secretary Kissinger in 1972 that led to a tremendous explosion in hard work and inward technology transfer on the part of Chinese.

In the United States, businesspeople awoke to a flood of goods from abroad making inroads on the US domestic market. The United States became an enormous importer of finished manufactured goods. What happened over the 1960s, 1970s, and 1980s through the consumption of imported goods was an enormous transfer of labor, of technology, of wealth, therefore of prosperity, from the United States to other countries.

The same thing happened in Europe and Japan: companies were undersold in their home markets by imports from countries where people worked hard, for long hours, for lower pay, but benefiting from technology and labor-saving practices now easily transferable from one country, one society, one culture, to another.

People entered the middle class around the world. What is middle class in Nigeria and Bolivia is not comparable to what is middle class in South Korea, but the thrust, the hunger for improvement, the money, and the means were in place.

A further change was virtually global improvement in farming technology. Better management of water, of crops, use of fertilizers, and sophisticated farm machinery brought about greatly increased food production, and with that, demand for better foods, more meat, and fresh vegetables. Better health care in the poorest countries led to lower infant mortality and, over the years, longer life spans in the more advanced countries.

The world became middle class together in the 1960s and 1970s to the great benefit of people growing up then, with the additional blessing of relatively few wars, only local ones, and the globe protected by treaties on nuclear weapons among at least the Soviet Union and the United States, Britain, and France. The reality of climate change was not yet obvious, and climate change as a political issue had yet to be discovered.

A further spread of technology came from US and European, and soon Japanese, multinational companies expanding into new markets.

For entrepreneurs outside of Europe, the US and Canada and Japan, three vital elements came together: technology, people, and funding.

For the United States, the newly globalizing world created opportunities for US multinationals and new competition inside the United States itself. Steel could be produced cheaper outside the United States than at home, and in due course that applied to all kinds of manufactured goods including cars and trucks.

Impetus came from the globalization of finance. In addition to the World Bank itself, whose task was to help economic development and raise standards of living, major European and American and Japanese banks greatly increased their activities. With increased offices on the ground and officers steeped in the culture and often language of host countries, the comfort level for making investments and taking risks increased. Banks and investment banks operated globally.

The United States and Europe prevailed in some industries such as aviation and advanced weaponry and semiconductors, Germany remained strong in motor cars and machinery, but for most consumer goods domestic production was substituted by far less expensive imports in large quantities to serve the needs of a growing, and demanding, middle-class American market. South Korea, China after the Nixon/Mao opening of 1972, India and Bangladesh, the Philippines, Vietnam, Mexico, Central America, and Brazil joined a long list of suppliers to the United States.

We in the United States enjoyed the prosperity; we bought the goods flowing in from manufacturers in other countries and imported into the United States, either as components or as finished goods, by our own businessmen.

What was missing in our drowsy perception of life around us was that as foreign suppliers replaced Americans, time-honored skills were lost in the

United States and plants that manufactured goods for the US market were no longer competitive.

Few paid attention to this slow-motion change.

The fact that the growing flow of imports into the United States was paid for by US dollars created by the Federal Reserve Bank also did not ring alarm bells. For the alert observer, an important change took place in 1965 when the US stopped issuing silver coins and instead issued US coins in cupronickel. In 1968 the US stopped redeeming silver certificate bank notes in silver.

These events were important signs on the road to taking tangible value out of the money we use for daily life and were accompanied by a period of high inflation and gradually concern about the value of the US dollar in silver and in gold.

During the 1980s and 1990s technology became far more widespread globally, and it was the application of technology to products and services that changed lives. The United States imported the things it needed from abroad with insufficient consciousness that there was a new world around us, able to compete in technology, able to develop new technology. The thinking among economists was that the United States was shifting away from a manufacturing economy to being a service economy.

In 2022 it is so obvious it no longer begs the question: cutting-edge industry and modern agriculture cover much of the earth, a startling contrast to the world in 1945 when the United States was the economic leader in technology and manufacturing for the world.

CHAPTER 10

Competition for US industry and growing US indebtedness

The United States had manufacturing competition from other countries by the beginning of the 1950s, starting in the early years with competition from countries that are today regarded as high cost.

As technological ability spread and manufacturing was done in increasing numbers of countries and over time in "developing" countries, the balance of trade changed. Other countries started to export more, including to the United States, and the United States started to export relatively less compared to emerging manufacturers elsewhere. During the years from 1950 on what started as a trickle became a stream and then a torrent.

The last year in which the United States had a positive balance of trade, meaning that exports from the United States exceeded imports from other countries, was 1975. In every year after 1975 and until 2022, the United States ran a negative balance of trade.

Once the US balance of trade turned negative, other countries paid attention and uncertainty about the backing of the US dollar followed. In 1976 and 1977 the United States was forced to issue some of its sovereign debt in Deutschmarks and Swiss francs in order to meet its financing needs.

The United States issued bonds, called Carter bonds, in Deutschmarks and Swiss francs, as a measure to protect the value of the US dollar. These were promises to repay borrowings in foreign currencies; a US government bond denominated in Swiss francs had to be serviced and repaid in Swiss francs. Foreign exchange risk at time of repayment was therefore removed from the lender and transferred to the United States Treasury. US debt had to be serviced and repaid in foreign currency, not United States dollars that could be created without limit on a printing press and by a bookkeeping entry on Federal Reserve Bank accounts.

The need for the United States to borrow in foreign currencies has long
since been forgotten and no one in the US Treasury is interested in reviving
that memory. Over the years the United States grew to be the world's largest
borrower in US dollars. As of now US sovereign debt, meaning the debt of the
US government, stands at $29 trillion.

Because the balance of trade of the United States has been unfavorable since
1975, US sovereign debt cannot be repaid by a surplus of exports. The trend is
the other way and getting larger all the time.

The surplus/deficit position is also affected by non-trade payments into US
dollars and out of US dollars, such as investments that foreigners make in the
United States and investments and non-trade payments that Americans make
in foreign countries. Those payments in, and out, either improve or worsen the
results. The balance of trade deficit for 2021 was US$1.09 trillion, the balance
of payments deficit was US$821.6 billion, indicating that non-trade payments
had a moderating favorable effect.

Growing borrowing by the United States will not be reversed. With few
exceptions like weapons and pharmaceuticals and aircraft, entertainment and
Internet services, we no longer are competitive in producing goods that other
countries and peoples want.

The balance of payments deficit each year is added to the pile of debt that the
US government owes, and the way that such debt is serviced and repaid is to
issue new debt. Interest payments on US government bonds and repayment of
US government bonds are done by issuing new US government bonds.

With increase of interest rates by the US Federal Reserve Bank, "the Fed,"
in 2022 and the great instabilities brought about by the Russian invasion of
Ukraine, the US dollar has increased in value in the short term, making it, at
present, more expensive for overseas buyers to acquire US goods and services
and, importantly, to repay debt denominated in US dollars. Any relief on the
US balance of payments front will be strictly temporary.

Government is different from you and me.

Imagine that situation in your own place of employment or your own household. No business, no family can continue to exist by indefinitely issuing new debt in place of the debt that it already owes. For a business, for a family, there must be repayment of debt. If there is no repayment or likelihood for repayment at a predictable time in the future, and if there is no security such as a mortgage on a house, debt is going to be called, and not renewed, and if unpaid, followed by legal action and ultimate bankruptcy.

When a family borrows, it is typically for a mortgage enabling it to put a roof over the family's head, for education of children, for autos, for furniture, all things that are needed for the family in life and for which, like a business, a return is expected in terms of improved financial stability over time, such as paying off a mortgage on a home. Family loans are repaid from salary earnings, successful businesses, and investment, and like a business, loans to individuals and families have to be serviced and repaid.

A business borrows to finance trade, purchases of goods for resale, receivables, assets, or salaries that will be put to use in the business, such as technology or investments in people or even other businesses, with the expectation that there will be a benefit, a return, on those investments that will enable servicing and repaying the debt plus the salaries of employees and a profit for the owners of the business.

Where is this headed?

What is different is that US government debt is incurred for living expenses of the nation, for imported things we consume, food, materials for housing and cars, clothing, and of course raw materials and components for manufacture of aircraft and weaponry.

Growing borrowing by the United States assumes willingness of domestic and foreign lenders to finance growing USA debt. An argument in favor of doing this is that "countries with spare funds have to invest in USA bonds and notes because they are the largest and most liquid market, and there is no other currency large enough and liquid enough to accommodate them."

That last phrase, underlined, is a dangerous assumption.

Our country is living on a giant "credit card," the balances of which grow larger all the time and which are repaid solely by issuance of new debt. As a country we depend on our ability to borrow to finance our living expenses, and we rely on the certainty of continued acceptability of the US dollar to make certain that we never have to repay what we borrow except by the issuance of further debt.

In 1971 the United States removed the convertibility of the US dollar into gold, an early warning to alert minds of a problem that had by then become insoluble.

There is a current in our country that is not interested in dealing with the reality of our ongoing debt and its continued acceptability as well as its effect on the population.

Thinking about this topic is very unpopular in the government. This issue needs thought by new minds: an individual who understands the issue and could be a powerful voice for action is economist Judy Shelton, who – unfortunately – is seen as a controversial political figure and was not confirmed on the Fed Board in 2021.

The situation has been worsened, understandably, through the huge increase in national debt to sustain people through Covid and more dollars chasing the same amount of goods, which has caused a large increase in inflation and a rise in interest rates.

No sensible household or business would live on debt that is steadily increasing and can never be repaid. The gradual slide into this financial management of our national life on a giant credit card is a soporific for which there has been no wake-up call so far.

A further aspect that has developed recently needs our attention: when sanctions were imposed on Russia following the invasion of Ukraine this year, it removed from the Russians the possibility of using the US dollar for its trade.

One of the attractions of the US dollar in international trade is its universality: that everyone who buys or sells can use the US dollar as a medium of payment. When a country is cut out of the US dollar system, the system itself becomes less attractive. Nations cut off from the US dollar find ways to use other currencies and work around what they consider as the tyranny of the US dollar.

When India buys Russian oil it conducts its trade in rubles; when Iran sells drones to Russia, it likewise uses rubles.

In restricting the use of the US dollar by imposing sanctions on countries, we reduce the universality of the appeal of the US dollar. As a country with high and growing indebtedness, the United States counts on the continued appeal of the US dollar for international payments as that permits an ever expanding amount of dollars. A very important part of that appeal is trust in the United States and its policies, which indirectly and unspokenly extend to the acceptability of its currency.

Reduced demand for US dollars would put the United States into a position where it would have to significantly raise interest rates or offer security, both highly unattractive paths.

What we would have to do as a country to control our debt is to increase our domestic investment, increase our exports of goods and services that are competitive in function, allure, price, and quality with goods and services available from other countries.

If this could be done on a massive scale it would work towards improving the trade balance into positive and gradually pay down debt. Improvement would come in small steps if the United States improves its productivity but in my opinion not enough to make a material difference.

Competition has become too great and our domestic US costs have become too high. We have lost the knowledge and the skills to manufacture many things that we have imported from other countries since many decades. Productivity is the key to competitiveness, and productivity has increased elsewhere while it has gradually declined in the United States for many activities.

Businesses need to improve their productivity because they are judged on their profitability, an excellent measure of effectiveness. They are held to account by their shareholders, accountability being a critical factor in the continued drive to be more productive, to improve, to be more competitive. Just as a business has to become more competitive, our nation has to become more competitive.

Reversing the negative trade balance at this point is unrealistic. Yet, in the absence of the ability to correct the trade balance we build in a permanent, enduring weakness, which is a danger for the nation.

A bright spot in the US picture has been the dynamism and expansion of American business, large businesses and small, banks and service companies. We have done a tremendous job in helping build our economy and the economies of other countries, bringing our technology, our values, and our management skills to bear.

Business has helped an explosion in human talent that has created prosperity at home. Abroad we have trained capable managers in other countries who in time often come to the United States to run American companies.

Our country and our leadership are primarily held to account by voters in terms of what their policies do for the recipients, the beneficiaries or otherwise of government policies.

It is dangerous to take our global status as a country for granted. We do not as a country have a burning desire to be globally competitive economically, and absence of that desire to be internationally competitive is a major weakness.

Our ability to create US dollars without limit that others are willing to accept insulates us for the time being from the reality of global economic competition, but circumstances, such as those described above, could cause that to change. For the time being, and especially since the Russian invasion of Ukraine, trust in the US dollar remains intact.

Our leadership is increasingly focused on domestic political, more than competitive economic, issues. Our view of the world outside the United States is substantially in terms of friends and adversaries or potential adversaries, in the geopolitical rather than the economic sphere because the US dollar is, for the moment, the leading international medium of exchange.

If our access to credit suddenly became very expensive or were cut off, for example if we through our own actions or adversaries outside the United States managed to dry up our access to borrowing, we would be in serious trouble.

Our indebtedness is the soft underbelly of the US economy. If an adversary, such as China, were able to wean the world off the use of the US dollar through the use of a government-issued crypto-renminbi, trade would be able to bypass the US dollar, and if on a large scale, the US would be in a situation where it would be hard-pressed to pay for its imports, consumption would be affected, and investment in the United States would be hurt. It is easy to imagine that China would have thought of this long ago.

What makes the US dollar survive as the leading international currency is the degree of confidence that holders of US dollars have in the United States. Despite the craziness of the Trump administration and the weakness and political partiality of the Biden administration, the United States will survive.

In the realm of trust compared to a digital renminbi the US dollar still looks good in the year 2022. China has increasingly one-person rule, reading the mind of Xi Jinping becomes a national and international preoccupation, so for the time being, a digital renminbi would not inspire sufficient trust to replace the US dollar.

We in the United States have some time, not forever, to improve our productivity, improve our national image of dependability, and thus strengthen faith in our US dollar and in our nation's future. Among the tasks at hand is the creation of a US government–issued, transparent, easily understood, digital US dollar that will in fewer years than we think replace the US dollar as we know it and use it today.

CHAPTER 11

Values and mindset

Starting in 1945 and to the end of the twentieth century the United States was accustomed to American economic global leadership in the mindset of the population of the country, even as realities around the United States started to change.

American values include taking for granted an assured standard of living for the country as a whole, which over time has hardly ever been objectively considered in our political discourse. We focus on inequalities within the system but not on our overall economic standard of living itself.

Our sense of entitlement to a predictable standard of living contrasts with the reality that, as a nation, we live on debt and no longer pay our way for many of the goods and services we consume as imports from other countries.

In the long-standing absence of a general increase in productivity in the United States, the actual standard of living has first leveled off, then declined, since the 1980s. If you do not believe it, you have not listened to persons working in manufacturing and in agriculture who saw their financial stability and security whittled away over the years.

Many things we do in the United States seem stuck in a time warp compared to normal practices in other developed countries. Much technology that could be improved if we enhance our productivity remains unapplied in the United States. That is true even at the level of the consumer in daily life.

In a restaurant in Europe, when a diner has finished and asks for the check, the waiter has a handheld machine into which the diner's credit card is inserted, it immediately verifies the validity of the card, a tip can be added if desired, and the diner gets his paper receipt immediately. The process takes a half a minute.

In comparison, in the USA we ask for the check, it comes, we hand over a credit card, and after a while the check returns with an imprint of the credit card, the diner adds a tip in ink, signs the debit, keeps a copy. This can take anywhere from five to twenty minutes if the restaurant is busy. Four or five interactions to pay one dinner check make it an unproductive use of a human being when technology could do the job. Machines to do this tedious job are at last being introduced in a few restaurants.

Our attitude to productivity often suggests that we believe that labor is readily available, and inevitable in much of what we do, whereas the opposite is true.

Human labor is scarce and valuable and precious. Productivity is what makes manufacturing and service processes efficient; it creates wealth and saves time and saves labor, thus freeing human labor to do more productive work that inherently is a better use of scarce human capacities.

Lack of advance in productivity is an important reason for inequality in the United States. Stagnant productivity condemns society to have persons employed in jobs where the future is limited. Limiting a person's future through lack of productivity constrains the possibilities of his or her contribution to society and, of course, limits earning power of individuals when someone remains in a low-level job.

Investments in productivity free people to tackle work where human involvement, effort, intelligence, and judgment are really needed.

There is no limit to human potential if we let the thoughts of our conditioning from the past fall away and grasp at betterment and opportunity for all of us as individuals.

Never underestimate others and their capacity if motivated and energized, and while you are looking at other people, never underestimate yourself. Seize opportunity, work intelligently and hard, contribute and deliver, and better yourself without fear.

CHAPTER 12

Ongoing role of the United States in the world wars and Pax Americana

The cold war between the Soviet Union and the West that started after World War II lasted to varying degrees until the fall of the Berlin Wall in 1989 and the collapse of the Soviet Union in 1991.

Soviet collapse in eastern Europe came about through a number of factors; the early revolt in 1956 in favor of freedom in Poland had a big part to play as did degrees of resistance in Hungary, Czechoslovakia, and even in East Germany.

Inside the Soviet Union the collapse came about through very gradual opening of society through the policies of *perestroika* (restructuring) and *glasnost* (openness) promoted by the late Mikhail Gorbachev, the last secretary-general of the Supreme Soviet, as well as through the weight of an inflexible centrally planned economy that no longer satisfied the requirements of late-twentieth-century life.

The United States had little to do with the collapse of the Soviet Union, though the collapse was seen as demonstrating the superiority of the Western economic system. One author, Francis Fukuyama, a political scientist affiliated with Stanford University, the author of *The End of History and the Last Man*, argued that the world had reached its political and social goal with the triumph of liberal democracy.

The end of the Soviet Union was seen by Fukuyama as being the end of history, a welcome political statement at the time. It was a perceptive view of the period from 1917 to the end of the Soviet Union in 1991 but a misunderstanding of the rise and fall of nations and cultures throughout history and of unpredictability of leaders and their ambitions.

History did not stop in 1991 and if liberal democracy seemed to triumph in 1991 it was a victory of short duration. Change lay ahead, and the United States would be part of it.

CHAPTER 12

Our wars have been costly, easy to start or to join, long and expensive to finish. Although other countries sometimes benefited, there was no economic benefit for the United States from the Korean war, the Vietnam war, the first Gulf war, the Kosovo conflict of 1998, the 2002 Afghanistan war, and the 2003 Iraq war to overthrow Saddam Hussein.

There were enormous human costs, loss of lives of American fighting men and later women, loss of life of inhabitants of countries where the wars took place, and great destruction of property.

Being the world's policeman was a costly exercise. On the positive side, the dominance of the United States in world affairs has, until fairly recent times, kept would-be aggressors in line, more or less assured the world that countries had to stay within their own borders otherwise the United States and its allies would take steps to ensure responsible behavior. This was Pax Americana, peace on American terms.

Billions of people were able to go about their lives, educate their children, and have a predictable geopolitical future because of Pax Americana, the security that the world enjoyed through the role of the United States in deterring aggression.

Highly noteworthy: during the years of Pax Americana since 1945 there has been no use of nuclear weapons by any country, a gift to all people by the United States, in the first instance, and by other possessors of atomic weapons like Russia, the United Kingdom, France, China, India, Pakistan, North Korea, and Israel, which deserves continued recognition.

The stability that the world counted on from Pax Americana is changing: examples of trouble ahead were the attack on Georgia by Russia in 2008, the seizure of Crimea by Russia in 2014, and very prominently, long term, was the publication by China of the "nine dash line" in 1949, after the Communists took over, appropriating to China large portions of the South China Sea beyond the internationally accepted twelve-mile limit.

By 1970 other nations started publishing their own claims to parts of the same South China Sea territory: Malaysia, Vietnam, and the Philippines. In 2016 the International Tribunal in the Hague, Netherlands, ruled that the "nine dash line" had no legal basis. China pointedly disregarded the ruling. In 2014, the year following Xi Jinping's assumption of power, China started building artificial islands inside the "nine dash line," heavily fortified and exclusively used for military purposes, with communications, aircraft, and missiles, thus enabling China to potentially control trade routes in the South China Sea and to project its military power into the Indian Ocean and to Australia.

A classic example of trouble ahead reminiscent of actions of Nazi Germany in the 1930s was the enormous buildup in 2022 of troops and military hardware in southern Russia and southern Belarus on the border of Ukraine, deeply threatening and ready at a moment's notice to attack Ukraine, which Russia wanted within its orbit of influence. In February 2022 that threat became a reality.

Democracies prefer to live in ignorance of threats as long as possible. To give the United States intelligence services credit, no nation wanted to believe that Russia would attack Ukraine, but Russia did start on February 24, 2022, with massive attacks from the south, Black Sea and Crimea, and from the east, Russia, and from the north where Russia had sent troops and equipment to Belarus. For the nations of western Europe, it was an unexpected wake-up call.

The easternmost countries of the EU that had formerly been in the Soviet orbit had a better understanding of the mentality of Russia and the risks, and they were right. Life changed forever in a few hours.

There is a connection between our American debt-fueled domestic economy and the results of our wars since the end of World War II. We would like to avoid foreign military engagements, if at all possible, and we aim to maintain our domestic standard of living by expecting that we will be able to borrow at a reasonable cost through issuance of US government bonds and notes.

This is a given that we take for granted. As stated in the previous chapter, the issues of competitive economies, lack of growth as a nation in the world context, the need to maintain our "middle class" standard of living to ensure domestic social tranquility all depend for the United States on unlimited access to affordable borrowing.

This translates into an important and unstated policy objective and related economic and military posture: though we do not announce it publicly, our

CHAPTER 12

objective and our actions as a nation are to maintain the status quo of our standing in the world.

This has been the unstated case for many years. With the passage of time, if our global competitiveness declines further, the need to maintain the status quo will become more obvious and more urgent. Without maintaining our competitiveness, in time we will be economically and militarily vulnerable in the eyes of the world. We will increasingly stand in front of other nations as a country that can be successfully challenged.

Much of this has been brought on ourselves. The Iraq war of 2003 is estimated to have cost the United States around $2.4 trillion, the Afghanistan war around $2 trillion. The result of the Iraq war was to depose and hunt down Saddam Hussein, who was not a threat to the United States, and to hand dominant influence in Iraq to the neighboring country of Iran, as the majority of Iraqis are Shia Muslims, as are Iranians.

Iran gained something for nothing, but this gift, at the cost of many American lives and many more Iraqi lives, did not increase the quality of our relationship with Iran, itself a far more powerful country than Iraq.

By long experience, the actions of the United States greatly matter, and if allies and adversaries see us behaving in an uncommitted and toothless way, they make their own judgment about how dependable we are in times of trouble. Adversaries understand that their margin for getting away with aggressions increases.

President Trump made the decision to close down US involvement in Afghanistan. Though President Biden claims he makes his own policy, he piggybacks on many Trump policies, both bad ones and good ones.

The most disastrous US international move during the Biden administration, so far, was the secretive, July 1, 2021,withdrawal at night from Bagram Air Base in Afghanistan.

It was not so much what the United States did in leaving Bagram, as how we did it, that sent a message to the Afghan military, which the US had trained and armed, that we were not a reliable partner and that there was no point in

CHAPTER 12

Afghans defending their own country. We showed the Afghan army and the Afghan government, by our actions, that it was time to leave if they could, because the Taliban would take over.

The Afghan army and Afghan government got the message. Takeover happened, far faster than the United States expected, with catastrophic results on August 30, 2021. American soldiers were killed, chaos prevailed at Kabul airport, and while some managed to leave, we left to their own fate thousands of Afghans who had helped the United States during the past twenty years, they and their families. As for Afghan women, their future was one of return to medieval times.

We carry the responsibility for this harm to the Afghan people through the way in which we left Afghanistan, the "how" rather than the "what."

It would have been possible for the United States in concert with the United Nations to establish a police force on the ground in Afghanistan of a few thousand soldiers to maintain the institutions and the systems of the then Afghan government in control.

Life in Afghanistan was not perfect but vastly better for the Afghan people and for Afghan women compared to what actually happened with having the Taliban, that we ourselves expelled from Afghanistan in 2002 for their support of the September 11, 2001, World Trade Center and Pentagon terrorists, back in power.

The actions of the Obama administration, the very different actions of the Trump administration, and later, the highly politicized actions of the Biden administration sent messages over the years to adversaries and allies alike that the United States was no longer a dependable international player.

Pax Americana was diminishing, no ally could count on the United States in the way it always had, and as for adversaries, testing time to probe American intentions was coming. It was understood over time that the United States would increasingly retaliate against unfriendly acts with legal and financial sanctions and not with military force.

That was a big difference from 1945. Change has come gradually as legalities and an inward-looking, divisive approach has replaced capable, courageous leadership and boots on the ground.

Taking only the comparison between the United States and China, looking at what happened to Pax Americana in a cultural sense, the United States is a young country behaving like an old country, concerned with maintaining its status and withdrawing from engagement. China is a very old country, behaving like a vigorous growing youngster, expanding, taking chances, certain of its coming dominance of the world.

Part III
Issues inside the United States

CHAPTER 13

Internal threats to the United States

The United States in 2022 is disunited.

Regional differences have given rise to political differences and differing values to a greater extent than at any time since the Civil War in 1861. Popular differences of opinion about joining the war in Europe on the side of the Allies in 1941 and opposing views on the Vietnam war in 1964 were minor compared to the opposing views the nation faces on many issues today.

There are many topics that fragment the country: perception of unfairness in income earnings and wealth, perception of gender inequality, of racial injustice, of abortion (pro-choice) or its prohibition (pro-life), the role of religion in ordering our society, the role of political bias in the media, the distance a nation may go to enforce Covid vaccination on the people as a public good versus the anti-vaxxers, to the right to carry weapons versus the move to ban assault guns, and identity labels ascribed, incorrectly and unfairly, to Black people, to Latino people, to white people, to LGBTQ people, to climate change believers, to mention a few.

The greatest threats to the United States are political divisions that are increasingly evident in this country, that pit red and the blue states against each other and that give rise to identity groups based on geography, gender, race, sexual orientation, and emotional topics like assault weapons. These give rise to dislike of groups of each other and influence battles over issues like education, rule of law, and law and order.

In the context of these differences and the mental harm caused by human detachment from others, there are increasing numbers of disturbed individuals taking matters into their own hands by attacking and killing innocent people in places of work and schools and stores with lethal weapons.

There is growing belief that we are not all in the same boat because wealthy people don't pay their fair share of tax. That said, politicians who make pronouncements about other people needing to pay their fair share don't point out that 32 million families file no income tax returns, and that in the year 2021 57 percent of the taxable population paid no federal income tax. Inequality is an issue not so much within communities but as a concept picked up by the right and by the left with different political solutions in mind.

In this month of October 2022 mid-term elections are less than a month ahead. Candidates for national office do much television advertising and it is notable that in 2022 candidate television advertising in the northeast of the country, where I live, focuses exclusively on negative qualities of candidates' opponents, without any claims as to candidates' own political objectives when in office. Everything is about how bad the other fellow, or woman, is and little or nothing at all about what the candidate himself or herself would do for the state or for the country. Such electioneering is unconstructive, highly divisive, and helps to promote dislike and hatred. It is a big step backward from the country that the United States needs to be.

Disappointing presidential leadership has been a contributor to divisiveness.

Because Americans nowadays often are urged to pick political sides, there is reluctance to stand back and look objectively at the jobs our presidents have done since 2001, the year of 9/11, a reasonable date to benchmark modern times.

Conspiracy theories originate mostly on the extreme right side of the political spectrum as an avenue to power and privilege for their authors. For those who believe in them, they are a lazy mind's way of addressing events, wanting to believe that the nation is run by manipulative groups instead of by people in a democratic society.

Conspiracies are largely untrue, but conspiracy theories do a great deal of harm. It is destructive and weakening to think that life around us is managed by conspiracies. Right-wing vigilante groups generate conspiracies of their own, a seed for great evil. Disturbed individuals often get their impetus for murderous acts of terror from imagined conspiracies.

Media both of the right and of the left contribute to worsening the political divisions and the perception of inequality of wealth and lifestyle. Media like CNN and Fox News unflinchingly support politicians they like, who receive nothing but favorable reports, or if their champion has committed a disaster, absence of much comment. Politicians they don't like never are given credit and are blasted even if they do good.

The week of May 3, 2022, marked the announcement of the alleged leak of a draft document from the US Supreme Court to overturn *Roe v. Wade*. The *New York Times* on May 4 made a festival out of this news, with the headline stretching clear across the front page and three pages in the inside of the paper dedicated to aspects of the story. What was potentially bad news for our country, in that it could deepen and intensify divisions, was a joyous windfall to this newspaper, which trumpeted that at last the Democrats had an issue that could win them the mid-term elections.

As perceptions blown up by media of right and of left harden, dislike and hatred by each of the other side increases. The media have much responsibility for the divisions in our country, and none of the media attempt to help unify us.

Where can one find a newspaper that doesn't tell lies and is not biased? It is the *Financial Times*, a United Kingdom newspaper simultaneously published in the United States and in a number of other locations around the world. Read it, and you will have the straight, for the most part unpoliticized story on events. Editorials are informative and educational, often with an unconventional view, though writers usually give a slant that can be seen as pro this or anti that. For those among us who want to see capable women in positions of power, the *Financial Times* did that just two years ago. The managing editor is a highly capable Arab woman, Roula Khalaf.

American media need to convince themselves that there is a need for unslanted truth, that media do not need to be politically biased, and that they have an enormous, positive contribution to make to the unity of our country. They don't have to run things the way they do today, as in how the *New York Times* on May 4 joyously celebrated the Supreme Court Justice leak.

CHAPTER 14

Disappointing Leadership

George W. Bush was elected president in 2000 and took office in January 2001, eight months before the terrorist attack on September 11 on the World Trade Center and the Pentagon. For much of his service he was a "wartime" president leading the country in recovering from the surprise attacks, inaugurating the justifiable 2002 war on the Taliban, who had sheltered Osama bin Laden and the terrorists in Afghanistan, then leading the country in the 2003 war against Saddam Hussein in Iraq.

In this second 2003 Iraq war Bush was encouraged by Vice President Dick Cheney and the so-called "neocon" group who believed that dominating Iraq would provide a source of cheap oil for the United States and Israel. Planning for the war was done with little regard for Iraq's history, its demographics, and its culture. The claim that Iraq had weapons of mass destruction proved untrue, greatly harming the reputation of an outstanding American, Colin Powell, damaged American credibility with its allies, and alienating France, which had a realistic view and better understanding of Iraq.

Though the 2003 war was a military success, It was costly in American lives and wounded, with an aftermath that cost hundreds of thousands of Iraqi lives. The war had the result of turning Iraq, previously ruled by minority Sunnis, to control by Shias that represented the majority of the country and the covert influence of Shia Iran.

Impetus for the 2003 Iraq war did not come from Bush alone. In the wake of 9/11, left and right on the US political spectrum were baying for blood, a chance to "hit an ugly face," that of Saddam Hussein and his supposed weapons of mass destruction.

Following the war when American occupation became unpopular in Iraq and unmanageable, leading in time to a civil war waged by extremist Islamists, many strong supporters of the war on the political left in the United States turned against it and claimed they had never been in favor.

CHAPTER 14

The 2003 Iraq war contributed to weakening the credibility and posture of the United States throughout the Middle East. Some US allies joined the effort but better informed ones like France did not. The 2003 Iraq war was the event most remembered about actions taken during the Bush presidency, a very big mistake with a bad outcome.

Bush led the enthusiasm for the war but it was not the sole fault of the administration; Congress and our people share the blame. Though the war cost the United States about US$2 trillion, we have not stopped paying for it as the ongoing problems from the Iraq war will be with us permanently.

Bush took no action when Russia attacked Georgia in 2008, a lack of objection watched carefully in Russia that helped set the stage for Russia's seizure of Crimea in 2014 and a visible step in the gradual decline of Pax Americana.

No objection amounts to tacit approval.

Barack Obama became president in 2009, winning over John McCain by a wide margin. His election was that of the first Black president of the United States, an important milestone in the history of our country and a big step forward in diversity. Though Obama had mostly domestic experience, he came to the job with high personal intelligence and the intention to do a good job for the country.

This very able man started out with much of the country behind him, but over time he was unable to work both sides of the congressional aisle and ended his second term ruling by presidential decree when he could not get his wishes passed by Congress.

Obama's presidency was a further contribution to erosion of the United States position in the Middle East: he made a notable speech in Cairo, Egypt, in 2009, during which he promised United States support for the Arab situation, but he did not deliver.

Domestically Obama helped pull the US economy out of the aftermath of the financial crisis of 2009, but apart from the lengthy and complicated and controversial Affordable Care Act, nothing major happened on his watch.

When Russia invaded and took over Crimea in 2014 Obama did not take US action. Obama was pacified by Putin and did nothing material to object to Putin's capture and takeover of Crimea, part of the nation of Ukraine. As in the time of George W. Bush, no objection amounted to tacit approval, and Russia duly took note.

Putin drew the correct conclusion about Obama, after Obama drew the wrong conclusion about Putin. The Ukrainians and the West and the United States are now paying the bill for the mistake of allowing Russia to seize Crimea.

Obama oversaw and led the world in the 2015 Iran nuclear nonproliferation agreement, which should have been stronger on the nuclear weapons side but more constructive in welcoming Iran back into good political odor globally, a missed opportunity both ways. Obama drew "red lines" for matters such as the use of chemical weapons in Syria, however when Syria crossed the red line, Obama did nothing, a great mistake resulting in a further loss of credibility.

Obama somehow balanced the immense weight of office with a personal life. He was a well-intentioned president who wanted to do the right thing but failed to act on the right things at the right time, taking the road of lesser resistance. Obama inherited from George W. Bush the ongoing debacle of the 2003 Gulf war.

The important contribution Obama himself made to our gently declining situation was the failure to maintain our strong, and essentially well liked, position in the Middle East.

The next presidential election was fought in 2016 between Hillary Clinton, the wife of former president Bill Clinton, and Donald Trump, real estate mogul and television personality, formerly a Democrat who switched to being a Republican.

Though Hillary Clinton and her husband former president Bill Clinton had ethics clouds in their background, Hillary Clinton had been secretary of state in the Obama administration, potentially more experienced and able than Donald Trump but divisive in her personality and her politics.

Hillary Clinton looked down on people who did not back her, going so far as to say that anyone not on her side was "deplorable" and should be doing "his fair share" of contributing by paying higher taxes. Some of the campaign tactics used against Trump were underhanded but characteristically, Mrs. Clinton admitted nothing.

People either worshipped Hillary Clinton or disliked her. She had the knack of getting peoples' backs up, not a good quality in a president.

Donald Trump had a vision. His instincts of what the country needed economically were good, and during his presidency the economy did well and there was a huge creation of jobs, and better jobs, for least advantaged people, for the most part done without throwing money at the problems. Lowering federal taxes made sense, although the underhanded hit against the Democrats was the capping of deductions for state and city income taxes, a blow below the belt against Democrat-voting states like New York, New Jersey, California, and Connecticut. Breaking a time-honored tradition, Donald Trump refused to make public his own tax returns as every previous president had since 1974 with the exception of Gerald Ford.

Highly divisive, everything was personal with Donald Trump; he came first, his supporters came next, the nation came as an occasionally benefited afterthought. Loyalty to Trump mattered more than loyalty to the job and to the nation. During his administration some around him were cronies and sycophants, others were extremely able people, who were often fired on a moment's notice if they expressed a view contrary to that of super-thin-skinned Trump.

A virtue of his administration at that time was transparency, especially in its negative aspects. If only because of the flood of adverse media coverage about Trump, it was possible to see day by day what was going on, who was in and who was out of favor, who was flying out the door, and there were actually pictures published of cabinet meetings.

Trump's bullying nature made it unattractive for capable, thinking people to stay in his administration. Conversely, Trump had natural admiration for "strongmen" such as Xi Jinping, Vladimir Putin, and Kim Jong-Un and a lukewarm attitude at best towards allies of the United States like Angela Merkel, chancellor of Germany, that he looked down on or disparaged. Trump pulled the United States out of the 2015 Paris agreement on climate change, out of the 2015 nuclear nonproliferation agreement with Iran, and out of the valuable Trans

CHAPTER 14

Pacific Partnership; that withdrawal was a self-inflicted wound for the United States, a defeat for USA allies in Asia and a welcome gift to China.

Drivers for most of these steps were Trump's desire to undo everything that Barack Obama had done, the good as well as the bad. Trump's self-centeredness and mean nature became United States policy and action. If adversaries had doubts about USA steadfastness during the Obama regime, those doubts got tremendous encouragement under Trump, seeing that the United States went out of its way to damage itself. US allies observed the petulance and changeability of Trump and his adoration of strongmen and understood that the USA under Trump would be an unreliable partner.

Trump was a practitioner of the "big lie," notable for his insistence that the 2020 presidential election, which he lost to Joe Biden, was stolen from him. That was and remains a lie; the election was conducted fairly and results in each state are tallied by local citizen volunteers who, whatever their personal political preferences may be, take their civic duties on the elections seriously. There is no "stuffing the ballot box" in the United States, and elections, with very few exceptions, reflect the public will.

Energized and wildly encouraged by his lie, armed Trump supporters broke into the US Capitol on January 6, 2021, in an effort to stop Vice President Mike Pence from declaring the election results in favor of Joe Biden. The attempt failed, not least that Mike Pence did his duty and called the election properly. The assault on the Capitol was the single worst day of my long life as a patriotic American citizen.

My vote for Joe Biden in the November 2020 election was for the lesser of two evils, without enthusiasm for Biden but the chance to get Trump out, and the departure from office of Donald Trump, whom I had voted for in 2016, was a relief.

Lack of enthusiasm for Joe Biden has been amply justified. A senator for many years, Biden was congenial and well liked and had served as Barack Obama's vice president. He had never been in an executive role, and in the wake of defeat of Hillary Clinton the Democratic Party had to pick a candidate that was mild and agreeable, an antidote to the unpredictability and self-centeredness of Donald Trump. In Biden they had that.

CHAPTER 14

A more different administration to that of Donald Trump can hardly be imagined. While Trump was all about advantage, openly and personally for all to see, in Biden it is not obvious. The story of Biden's son Hunter in Ukraine is illuminating: Hunter Biden was selected to be a board member of Ukrainian company Burisma, whose business he knew nothing about, at a compensation of US$50,000 per month, an amount that exceeds the annual earnings of many Americans.

It is hard to imagine what value Hunter Biden added to the board of a Ukrainian company whose business he did not know, except for his connection to Joe Biden.

That Trump loathed and feared Joe Biden in the 2020 presidential election was clear: he had his adviser Rudy Giuliani, the former mayor of New York who wrecked his reputation serving Donald Trump, dig up dirt on Hunter Biden and Joe Biden to hurt Biden's election chances. Trump vitriol on Biden sleaze was not a pretty sight.

Biden's cabinet choices are made in the interests of diversity. Every identity group is represented, some of a strong left-wing persuasion, but of the cabinet itself and its workings, nothing is seen, nothing is heard.

Biden has been president now for nineteen months, I have yet to read a single report of a cabinet meeting or see a single picture of the Biden cabinet meeting at work. No transparency, no communication, and I wonder when they meet and what they do.

Even Kamala Harris, our vice president, after having been assigned some unattractive assignments that were likely to fail, has disappeared in photographs from her demure seat to the right and rear of Joe Biden, who now appears mostly alone.

Biden's thinking is slow, though he occasionally comes out with emotional remarks that stick to him until aides do their best to unglue him and attenuate the impact. As to policies, Biden is guided by an unseen hand that steers him leftwards, in favor of massive, vote-getting spending of money the United States does not have.

CHAPTER 14

Biden has been a failure in unifying the country, just as Trump was a failure, each in his own distinctive way, but their failure to unify us means that the country and its citizenry has paid, and is now paying, the price of their failure.

I give our secret services great credit for spotting Putin's intentions on Ukraine ahead of other nations, and I give Biden credit for announcing them. It is one thing that Biden has done well, but even that went nowhere at all compared to the disaster of our pullout from Afghanistan and the message it sent to the world.

Though Biden electioneered as a president for all Americans, he has been unsuccessful in unifying the country. Many Democrats have a poor opinion of his presidency. I doubt that Biden is capable of thinking through high-level policies for our country for the medium and long term. On the rare occasions when she appears, First Lady Dr. Jill Biden makes a good impression.

Who might Biden's invisible "minders" be? How and when and where does Biden meet with them, and how do they influence and direct Biden policy? They seem deliberately low-key; they do not show their hand.

I suspect that the Biden minder clique includes among its tasks the diminution of Kamala Harris, for fear that she may be the chosen Democratic candidate in the 2024 presidential elections. Harris is not far enough to the left for their tastes, and she has been a district attorney with a duty of promoting law and order, out of fashion among the extreme left.

Of the three presidents after George W. Bush, Obama was the best. However, the succession of Obama, Trump, and Biden added up to a chain of weak leadership, each different from the other, but their individual regimes and the three together were damaging for the United States and intensified the divisions among us.

Look at the state of disunity today and it is obvious.

CHAPTER 15

Disunity is weakness and strength begins at home

While China is becoming a more influential power globally, and Russia is attempting, through violence, to re-create its empire of the past, we in the United States are preoccupied with ourselves, focusing on our past rather than our future, sharpening divisive emotional attitudes from one part of society and from one part of the country to another.

Only a society that thinks of itself as safe and well-off can indulge in such wasteful luxury. The feeling of safety and taken-for-granted prosperity is a very unsafe illusion.

For allied countries that believe in and practice freedom and democracy as well as for the United States itself, our American preoccupation with ourselves, self-absorption, and divisiveness are dangerous realities.

We are the authors of these high-risk problems and our leadership in recent years, each in different ways, has contributed to the divisions in our country.

The unprovoked attack of the Russian army on the nation of Ukraine on February 24, 2022, was a wake-up call. It was the first nation-unifying event in the United States since the attack of 9/11, twenty-one years ago.

Most Americans are moved by the senseless destruction of Ukraine's cities, by killing of innocent citizens, displacement of millions, and by the steadfastness and readiness to risk their lives for their country of Ukraine President Volodymyr Zelensky, the Ukrainian army, and the Ukrainian people.

We admire the resistance of the Ukrainian people in response to an unprovoked attack.

Can we imagine the United States in such a situation as that of Ukraine? Would we pull together as a nation despite the divisions that take center stage today?

The attack of 9/11, 2001, and the 2022 attack of Russia on Ukraine were externally driven events, terrorist actions on the United States in the case of

CHAPTER 15

9/11 and threats and violent assault on a friendly democratic country in the case of Ukraine.

Do we want unity forced on us by an attack against the United States or against allied countries, or are we willing to bridge differences and strengthen our unity?

Except for the Ukraine war and growing external threats what we see around us in 2022 is inward-looking and divisive. As a result of shrill efforts of extreme right and extreme left to push identity-based agendas, it becomes difficult for Congress and the administration to formulate and enact policies that are for the common good.

What can you and I as citizens do about divisiveness?

When you observe or are pressed to join a drive to gain support for a cause-based or an identity-based faction, stand back from the emotional rush that the promoters seek to create in you and ask yourself the question, "who gains from this?"

The individuals who gain are not potential supporters like you and me to whom appeal is made for adherence and money but the individuals who lead the shrill factions, who seek money from contributions and political power for themselves.

Their appeal is not for your benefit; it is for their benefit.

Consider what is being promoted and use your common sense. Factions that seek to create identity associations, links through emotional excitement, and a feeling that you have been wronged or a feeling that you are weak without their guidance will benefit the organizers.

Identity associations seek to crystallize identities, dictate to people what they need to believe and how to live, divide citizens from each other and in the process they hurt the United States and its people. Be suspicious of electioneering that only seeks to paint the opponent in an unflattering light and says nothing about the candidate herself or himself.

CHAPTER 15

In a divided and potentially antagonistic environment, our federal government is faced with political factions making demands for attention, working to capture the center of each party for the support and endorsement of at times extreme programs.

Step back, and look at our country from a height of 36,000 feet.

The values of people in the broad center of the Republican Party and the people in the broad center of the Democratic Party are not far apart: people of all political persuasions want life, liberty, and the pursuit of happiness; a good standard of living; a safe and prosperous future for their children and their country; and they are willing to work for these things. These are shared values of the American center, a force for good.

We whose future is at stake need to reach consensus among ourselves rather than to have our unity forced on us by a catastrophe such as a war against the United States or disastrous secession of part of the country that some extreme people actually favor.

The center matters and it is the key to our future as a nation. Understanding the need for unity and promoting unity together around common values in a competitive world where our position as a nation matters is your task and my task.

CHAPTER 16

Political correctness as a contributor to weakness

From September 11, 2001, forward to 2022, there has been a change to thought control, led by rigid liberal thinkers, who are not liberal at all but highly restrictive in their desire to regiment views and speech on the left, as well as by rigid, at times fanatic, conservatives on the right.

Extreme liberals and extreme conservatives are both to blame, and those in the middle ground of both Republican and Democrat Parties share the blame when they lose their bearings and fall victim to extreme persuasion themselves in the search for votes.

Extreme liberals promote "political correctness," a great danger to the development of educated and able and competitive young people. The best universities are among the worst offenders in the movement to restrict and control thought, to stifle and remove views that are not in line with their "politically correct" thinking.

That is perfectly exemplified by my own university, Princeton, which publishes the magazine *Princeton Alumni Weekly*. The October 2021 issue contains the welcome speech of university president Christopher L. Eisgruber to the incoming class of 2025. Much of his talk is dedicated to a medical issue of his own and how that medical problem underlines the existence of weaknesses and imperfections in himself and others.

The specific issues the president raises to new students starting their university education are "important and emotionally charged topics such as race, sexuality and justice." Nowhere in President Eisgruber's speech is there any reference to freedom of thought, to freedom of speech, to openness and transparency, to the universality of learning, or to the situation and future of the United States.

I make a degree of allowance for President Eisgruber in that he is surrounded by a community that is itself enamored of political correctness. Nonetheless, President Eisgruber's talk has an inward-looking and apologetic tone, dwelling on the combination of frailty and aspiration in people, including in the new students.

CHAPTER 16

In this talk from one of our leading academics, President Eisgruber exemplifies what is leading the United States to be globally uncompetitive: that inward looking matters most and that the important issues are those that affect our identities as people.

There is nothing in his speech that reflects the long-standing Princeton ethic of contribution, of helping to make the world better, "Princeton in the nation's service." That time-honored ethic is never mentioned.

The best universities of the eastern United States are comparable to Princeton in their desire to channel political thinking.

A by-product of political correctness is this: foreign students, a huge source of income for American universities whose foreign graduates may carry positive thoughts about the United States throughout the world for the rest of their lives, come to the United States for the best in universal education. Foreign students want exposure to freedom of thought, where all opinions may be heard; they do not want to come for teaching that is ipso facto restricted to "non-dangerous" politically correct ideas from the start.

Political correctness hurts the appeal of American universities to non-Americans, which diminishes the lasting good for our country from foreign graduates who studied here.

Politically correct thinking supports the efforts of those who would like to rewrite our nation's history, to do it all differently, as if it had never happened. But since it did, to push our collective noses into the dirt to make certain that we take every bit of it in.

In its history the United States is like other nations: it has done much right and some wrong. Our history has reflected the views and acts of the people then in charge and the mood and culture and habits of the population at the that time. Sometimes they did things that are abhorrent. George Washington owned slaves, and we have to accept that he did. His ownership of slaves reflects the time in which he lived and ruled the country.

Within seventy years after George Washington, the North of the United States went to war with the South to eliminate slavery. That Civil War, at a tremendous cost in human life in both North and South, 360,222 dead in the Union Army and 258,000 dead in the Confederate Army, was followed in 1865 by the abolition of slavery.

If the American people owe a debt to the persons suffering enslavement in this country before abolition of slavery, the 360,222 dead in the Union Army is a considerable down payment on that debt, paid 157 years ago in blood and lives and suffering of families.

That terrible death toll and the absolute determination of President Abraham Lincoln to rid us of slavery were essential steps in the elimination of this abominable curse. No other country suffered such a loss of life in the just fight to eliminate slavery.

The payment of financial indemnities to the descendants of Black people who were enslaved may be soothing to the moral sensitivities of the giver, such as Harvard University, which has announced a gift of US$100 million for this. The gift does nothing for those descendants themselves and cements further divisiveness, correcting nothing that happened over a hundred and fifty years ago, and deepening the crisis of identity.

To rid the United States of the foul aftermath of slavery, the impoverished condition of former slaves and the cessation of the color bar in education and in public places took another eighty years. There are still today ways to discourage eligible minority people from voting. That does not reflect well on us and must be changed so that all citizens have an easily registered vote.

We have to look the consequences of our past deeds in the face, recognize that along with the bad there were many accomplishments and remarkable, extraordinary growth as a nation. As a nation we were widely and broadly admired; we ourselves should respect that admiration and take pride in it. We have to move beyond the past into the future.

Nothing in the past can be changed. We cannot rewrite the past but must recognize it, accept it, and move on together in unity to a better future.

The universities, especially the best ones such as Princeton, have duties to the nation and to mankind from which there is no escape: they have to be a forum for learning everything to do with the human condition, our past, our future, and our universe. Everything means everything: all ideas have to be accessible, all books, all teachers, all visiting speakers. Universities should not pick and choose books and teachers and visiting speakers depending on their own "politically correct" preferences.

Faculty and administration should constantly, repeatedly emphasize to the students that openness to all ideas, all books, all visiting speakers is encouraged; they have to think that way, they have to talk the talk and walk the walk, lead by example of openness, of acceptance of the value of the universe of knowledge. Students attend universities so to be able to form critical judgments of their own and not so that they adhere to a thought standard dictated by faculty or administration.

Openness to read everything and to listen to people even if one disagrees is part of the culture of understanding, learning, and wisdom one expects of a university. Banning and removal of books that are out of favor, harassment and repudiation of speakers and professors saying things that are politically not in favor must itself be forbidden.

Books have to be treated with respect, as they are a part of the author who wrote them, and visiting lecturers should always be treated with the courtesy that is accorded a guest in one's home irrespective of whether the majority of students and faculty agree with the speaker's viewpoint or not.

"Safe spaces" where topics and ideas are prohibited, banning of speakers who disagree with the administration, are an infringement on liberty and an assault on learning.

A university is there to expose its students to all of the learning possible, and then let the students form their own opinions on what is just, constructive, positive, and makes sense. Anything less equates university education with book burning in Nazi Germany in 1935. Intellectual control by "political correctness" is a terror of its own.

As an institution of learning, a university teaches and graduates students who are future builders of the nation and of the world. That is among its important responsibilities, and that means building an inclusive sense of community, understanding that all viewpoints have value and matter, fostering a culture of readiness to listen to others and building bridges to them, and that one's duty includes contribution to the nation and to society.

CHAPTER 17

Educating our young people

The performance of American fourth graders, eighth graders, and high schoolers ranks far behind that of other countries. Generally speaking, we rank thirteenth in reading in the world behind countries such as Russia, Taiwan, Singapore, Poland, and four provinces of China.

The results in mathematics are worse; USA students are ranked thirty-sixth out of seventy-nine countries worldwide. Not so fast! The US Department of Education says it's not that bad: the real ranking of US students is better; it is thirtieth out of seventy-nine.

That ranking, thirty out of seventy-nine, instead of thirty-six out of seventy-nine, is not any consolation and should make us feel profoundly dissatisfied.

The National Assessment of Educational Progress recently announced a drop in reading scores, the biggest drop since 1990, as well as the first drop in mathematics scores, and that the decline in scores is worse among disadvantaged people.

Other subjects rank even worse: one statistic that is well known is that many high schoolers, 11 percent of all, cannot locate the United States on a map of the world, 29 percent cannot find the Pacific Ocean, and 63 percent cannot find Iraq on a map of the Middle East. US student performance in history is even worse, leaving aside the current chaos created by the efforts of some people in rewriting and expunging parts of our history.

With scores such as these our students are being badly equipped to compete in a highly and increasingly competitive world.

The difference in quality of education in this country from one city and town to another is breathtaking. Schools in major cities whose students are from poorer families, Black or Latino, are disadvantaged, whereas students from suburbs and wealthy towns have far better quality schooling and as a result are better educated.

CHAPTER 17

Inequality of schooling is a bigger problem in the United States than inequality of wealth for the reason that inequality of schooling is a permanent hindrance to the disadvantaged that cannot be easily corrected.

How do we compete globally as a nation if our young people are not competitive in math, science, reading, writing, computer skills? How can our young people be an effective part of the world if they cannot master geography, history of regions and countries, the influence of religions and cultures, and key industries in their own country and other countries? We send our young people to adulthood ignorant of basics.

In order to be a competitive player in the world, the United States needs better quality elementary, junior high, and high school education for all, not just for those living in privileged communities.

Schools in underprivileged communities have to be just as good in their teaching, held to the same high standards, as those in wealthy communities. If we can do that we will have a level playing field where people of all races and national origins and economic backgrounds will have an equal, high-quality start. That is the United States that we must be for all of our young people and the future of the nation.

This may be the most difficult single task that the country has to face, but there are early signs that people are taking note of the problem and want to do something about it.

The tide is turning against issues like renaming of schools in the interest of "political correctness" and "critical race theory," distractions that draw attention away from basic skills like reading, writing, math, science, geography, history, computer science, languages, and economics that young people need.

We must teach our young people the basics, and we have to do it thoroughly and well.

The biggest potential ally in this task are in the early years, the parents of students, and as young people grow up, the students themselves. Parents want their children to be properly equipped for life in a competitive world, and young people want to do well themselves. Given a chance, everyone is on the side of success.

Schools should be managed by communities, not by the national government, because communities have the strongest and closest interest to ensuring that young people are well educated. States are the overseers of communities and responsibility by states for the good education of their young people is critical. Competition among schools is constructive, so charter schools and church schools have a role to play in ensuring that public schools are of a high standard and are competitive in results of their students.

Where the federal government should come into education is to ensure excellence, high standards for all, in all fifty states, to publish standings of the United States versus other countries, making this a topic of concern and popular consciousness and debate, and to improve our national ranking. Our ranking among the world's nations should be an important part of the national dialogue, and year by year, we should seek to improve our standing.

We should never lower standards to give the appearance of making academic achievement attainable in the interest of promoting disadvantaged people.

The way to benefit disadvantaged people is to have truly excellent schools for all and the same high standards for everyone. We all need to be strongly encouraged, through excellent local schools, good teaching, and nurturing, to learn and to achieve.

If we keep standards high, we will not be disappointed.

Hardworking and motivated young people of all races and religions and backgrounds, advantaged and disadvantaged and those in the middle, will not only meet high standards but will blow away the targets.

Teachers have to be held accountable for the results of their students. Teachers, like all of us in every walk of life, have to be judged on what they accomplish, and that means the motivation, encouraging, caring, and coaching of students, so that their students attain the good results that they themselves need and that our country needs.

CHAPTER 17

Fortunately most teachers, including those in public schools and teachers that are unionized, are dedicated people devoted to the education of their students. School boards and unions that protect occasional poor teachers harm young people and hurt the future of the country. There is no excuse for that, no matter how much political power a school board or a teachers' union may have. Parents and communities must act to change school boards and teachers that don't do a good job of educating young people.

CHAPTER 18

Gender equality

Talent and ability are scarce and we need all the talent and ability we can enlist if we are to survive in a competitive world. If one were to assume, roughly, that 50 percent of the US population is born male and 50 percent is born female, irrespective of whether they were born in the United States or abroad, it is imperative that we address 100 percent of the population universe as we seek to fill jobs that are needed for our nation to compete.

Addressing 100 percent of the universe may seem a logical first step, but one has to go farther. It is essential in the interest of diversity that men and women have a realistic shot at every position, that there be no distinction regarding eligibility on the basis of gender.

It is long since past time to think that only men should have the important jobs at work, in management, and on boards of directors, in academia, in the professions, in government. Everything has to be truly open to everyone. Good ethics, teaching ability, knowledge, and dedication should drive choices as to whom to elect and how to fill jobs.

Why is that so? A diversified organization does a better job. It enlists more kinds of talent, of life experience, more mentalities, and the more different kinds of people there are in an organization, be it a business, a professional office, a school, or a government, the better a job it will do. Diversity works. Narrowness and identity of views, coziness and cronies, are a hindrance.

The world has been male dominated throughout history, with a very few exceptions, and only in the twentieth century and the twenty-first century have women started to make real progress in equaling their participation and contribution to that of males at every level. At the top level, the president of the United States, the USA is still an outlier compared to the United Kingdom, Germany, Bangladesh, India, Sri Lanka, New Zealand, Denmark, Estonia, Switzerland, France, Sweden, Finland, Chile, and Argentina, each of which had or has a woman as president or prime minister.

What is needed is both men and women and their access and availability for all kinds of tasks, especially including leadership.

The search for talent and capability in the 100 percent universe should include transgender people, with the same level playing field as for men and women. People must be selected for positions based on their abilities and their character, not on their gender or whether they are transgender. The quality of the individual counts, not their gender.

There is no justification for paying people differently on the basis of gender, or race, or religion. If that was done by some employers in the past, it is time to stop that and to pay for work equally, irrespective of who is performing the work.

There is a right that applies to the female gender and that is the right to an abortion if a woman so chooses. Women have the right to the ownership of their bodies. That was granted forty years ago at a national level by the *Roe v. Wade* decision of the US Supreme Court, and for the sake of our population it must remain in force. The vast majority of citizens want that right ensured and underlined at a federal level.

How can we imagine removing from a person a right, not harmful to society or to others, that she or he already has? It is an assault on that person's freedom.

We have no right to impose our beliefs on others, but we do have a duty to protect the freedom of choice of every person, always provided that it does not do harm to anyone else who is already born, alive on earth, and a sentient being.

The decision for a woman as to whether or not to have an abortion is already sufficiently complicated. It may be divisive and emotional and wrenching, it may or may not leave permanent emotional scars; let us, the citizenry, not make it more difficult by passing laws telling people what they can do, and what they cannot do, with their own bodies.

These rightful measures are all steps in making certain that the United States has access to the entire universe of people in addressing its global competitiveness. Everyone is needed as a candidate in nation building and creating a fair society: male, female, lesbian and gay, transgender, people of every race and religion that are part of this society. Everyone is welcome, everyone is needed, and understanding and practicing this will be a great help to our unity as a nation.

CHAPTER 19

Absence of connection
The coincidence of Covid and technology

Covid was discovered in China and started spreading in late 2019 and early 2020. By January 2020 there was a recognized problem, though the extent of it and the likely spread was not yet obvious. Covid was recognized as a pandemic on March 11, 2020, and with that, lives changed quickly.

Restaurants, businesses, schools, and public spaces were places where people could contract Covid, and without medical protection people started getting sick and filling the hospitals. Medical staff got sick. Elderly people were the most likely to have respiratory problems; there was a shortage of hospital ventilators. Many people died, especially in nursing homes.

At the same time technology was enabling people to work from home. For restaurants, retail stores, and travel, Covid was a disaster that wrecked business. In many countries around the world including the United States, companies that could do so encouraged their people to work from home, come to places of work minimally, and Zoom and Microsoft Teams meetings became commonplace.

The coincidence of Covid and work-from-home technology added distance between us, reduced engagement, and contributed to the divisiveness harming our country.

Through this conflation of Covid, technology, and the subsequent higher risk of contracting Covid by living in cities due to large populations, many people who could moved to suburbs and to rural areas, using their Internet connections to work from home. Schools taught their lessons online and some closed, so a new era of home schooling started for millions of parents. Many people lost their jobs, and fortunately the US and many other governments came to their partial rescue with cash support.

Most people greatly reduced their social interactions with others, even with their own families, in hunkering down to protect themselves and their families from Covid. Parents started a new way of life, in many cases forcibly working from home, spending much more time on child care and children's education. Company Zoom meetings often included children at work or play in the background of employees' homes.

In late 2020 the first vaccinations had been developed and tested – credit the amazing speed of Pfizer and their German partner BioNTech and of Moderna – to be followed soon by a Chinese vaccine, a Russian vaccine, and AstraZeneca and Johnson & Johnson vaccines.

In countries of the West and developing countries that could afford the vaccines, progress was uneven and dependent on politics. In the poorest countries vaccination was the slowest. Covid progressed wherever people were unvaccinated, including among "anti-vaxxers" in Western countries.

Fast-forward to September 2022 in the United States: some people still wear masks in public places, others do not despite reports of a resurgence of Covid. Whenever and wherever there has been a lack of attention, or deliberate inattention, to vaccination, to masking, to handwashing, the numbers of cases rise, particularly as temperatures drop. People become frustrated with protective measures, and people congregate unmasked as we do on holidays.

Offices have cautiously or in some cases, incautiously, reopened; the mentality of employees has changed. Some employees miss the interaction and engagement of being in an office in person, others do not, and of those, many feel that they have a right to work partially or entirely from home.

What people have gone through as a result of diminished engagement with others is a first in the lives of every person alive, with the exception of the few aged over one hundred who lived through the epidemic of the Spanish flu in 1918–1920.

Unless people are in solitary confinement in prison or in isolation for religious purposes, we are used to being with other people from early in the morning throughout every day.

Covid fundamentally changed our social interaction. Individuals may have gone through a day being only with immediate family, the only outside contact being a person who delivers food, if one is fortunate enough to be able to arrange it. In Shanghai and other cities in China where there is a rigid policy of Zero Covid, that isolation has been an enforced requirement, with severe punishment for breaking the system.

Our behavior as people has fundamentally changed. As we gradually return to a semblance of normalcy, many of us yearn for more person-to-person contact; we miss daily and multiple interaction with others. Conversations in the post office or the supermarket are often more connected than in the past; we want to know more about each other and we want to see more of each other. That is not easy in a world of telephone menus and tasks being handled electronically.

Covid got technology off to a supercharged boost; Covid may, hopefully, decline, but the technological changes that Covid encouraged will remain with us, will strengthen, and become greatly enhanced in the years ahead. Inevitably that means a further drop in individual-to-individual contact.

Add that to the large amounts of time that people spend on the Internet including playing electronic games, and the increased detachment from other people becomes obvious. Young people who master electronics yet maintain their connection with other, real-life, human beings, not avatars, are extremely fortunate, and society shares that good fortune.

Not everyone is so lucky. The effect of the drop in interaction with other people is a serious matter that has yet to play out. Whatever one's view, being separated from other people in business and in society for two years has had an effect. Some children have slipped behind in their learning so they now have a lot of catching up to do. This has been especially true in disadvantaged sections of our society.

Some adults and many children have felt lonely, alienated, likely to suffer from depression, and may need psychiatric care. Depression has spread. With less engagement with others at work, in restaurants and shops, at church, people are inevitably less connected to other people than they were before Covid.

In-person engagement is a factor in building a sense of responsibility to each other, appreciation for the other person, and a degree of understanding for the needs and desires and problems of other people. This massive loss from the coincidence of Covid and technology has not even begun to be understood.

From person-to-person engagement with others comes responsibility to others. From responsibility comes accountability, and from accountability comes trust.

Trust is the quality that keeps us going, that makes life dependable, that is our solid faith in institutions, in the leadership of our businesses, including our own bosses, and in the leadership and faithful representation of our senators and congresspeople, and of our president and cabinet. Relationships work better if they are real, in person, and not on Zoom or Microsoft Teams. Online communication may capture the substance of what is discussed but the human side is partially lost.

Lack of person-to-person engagement helps alienation and depression and suicidal thoughts develop, through diminished responsibility to others and to institutions. In 2022 there are reports of persons accepting jobs and not turning up when they committed to start work, a reflection of lack of responsibility for the mutual commitment that has been made, greatly adding to the feeling and reality of a divided society.

Zoom is great, Microsoft Teams is great, but they cannot compare to truly being together in person with other human beings. If the metaverse becomes a reality, the involvement of avatars instead of real people will be a further deterioration of engagement compared with Zoom and Microsoft Teams, a step back from being together with real people. Avatars will make engagement, mutual responsibility, and accountability harder and trust will inevitably suffer.

We need to reconnect at school, at work, at church, mosque, and synagogue, in stores, in shops, at weddings and funerals, at the post office, and at the car dealership. Connection with people is a basic human need, we all need it, and we should engage for the joy of it, for the engagement, for the contribution to ourselves and to our society and our nation. Engagement is a must and engagement with others helps build the unity of our country.

Part IV
The United States
and the world

CHAPTER 20

The perception of our military power and willingness to use it

Compare the United States today to the situation of the country during the Vietnam war, which lasted from 1955 to 1975, becoming increasingly controversial during its time. There were serious objections to the war. Unusual in the United States, the military did its job in the field but faced lack of support at home.

Many Americans felt that there was no reason for the United States to be in Vietnam and some men sought to avoid the draft.

This did not happen during the first Gulf war in Iraq in 1991, nor in the 2002 war in Afghanistan, nor the second Iraq war launched in 2003. There has been no draft into the military since 1973, though men reaching the age of eighteen are still required to register for selective service. Women reaching eighteen are not required to register, despite the role of women being part of combat having been changed in 2015.

The population was behind the 2002 war to eliminate Al Qaeda in Afghanistan and enthusiastic about the 2003 war in Iraq to eliminate Saddam Hussein. Few Democrats or Republicans were against the 2003 invasion of Iraq, much as some politicians squirm and try to deny it today.

It has been part of American culture to admire and respect the military, with particular appreciation for the soldiers, now gender blind, who risk their lives in defense of the country and its interests. Through good times and bad times, the army, the navy, and the air force, and each of their academies, West Point, Annapolis, and the Air Force Academy, enjoy popular support and respect. This is an enormous blessing, which we never take for granted, despite fallible political leadership.

At the same time our military understands that they are under the orders of a civilian president and are responsible to the people. How very fortunate that this is so, another American attribute that is far from universally true around the world.

My recommendation to my fellow citizens is to honor our military and to prize its subordination to the president and civil society.

Never take this subordination for granted.

A strong military, respected by the nation, ready to do the needed work of our country and equipped with state-of-the-art, cutting-edge equipment and technology is essential for the defense of the nation and its allies and for our future.

This is as true in 2022 as it ever was, and if we take account of the increased presence of "strongmen," autocrats like Vladimir Putin who attack neighboring countries, it is more important than ever.

Just as the greatest internal threat to the United States is its divisiveness, the greatest external threat to the United States is the loss of the global perception of American strength and determination on the part of the United States to defend its interests, with military action if necessary.

The United States took a notable step in the change for the worse of perception through its secret, by-night evacuation of Bagram Air Base in Afghanistan on July 1 last year. That was followed by chaotic exodus from Afghanistan on August 30, 2021, after spending nearly twenty years on the ground there, backing the Afghan government, and promoting a social structure that enabled a decent life for Afghan women and a future for the country.

Our good standing and image in Afghanistan and the $2 trillion we spent on the war effort there evaporated in weeks. It was not the "what" of our leaving Afghanistan but the "how" it was done that mattered and the misery that we left behind.

The United States is not associated with panicked, hasty, disorganized exits and this one was notable and out of character.

It is unfair to blame the US and allied military for the mess; it was not their doing, it was politics, starting with Trump's decision to withdraw and ending with disastrous execution under Biden.

Arm's-length reflection would have concluded that a relatively small contingent of US and allied forces, likely augmented by a United Nations contingent, could have kept Afghanistan stable, the Taliban out, and Afghan people free to be well educated irrespective of gender and to develop their country for generations from now.

In doing this we would have delivered on an implied promise made when we first supported Afghanistan after the war of 2002 that removed the Taliban from power.

Instead, today the Taliban are back in charge.

We ask the Taliban rulers who harbored the terrorists that attacked us on 9/11 and that we kicked out in 2002, in a polite way, to please do things to accommodate our needs on an exceptional basis. Meanwhile the Afghan economy is dead in the water and Afghan women do not have normal rights.

Much of the disaster was avoidable. As we read stories of how women in Afghanistan are now deprived from education and cannot travel without a male escort, we have to look our failure in the face. We are responsible for a mess that should never have happened. Had we done what we should have, the Afghan people would have stability, continuity, and a future, and America's reputation in a difficult part of the world would have been enhanced. In money terms, we would not have seen the two trillion dollars that we spent in Afghanistan go to waste.

Observing our behavior in leaving Afghanistan, even long-standing allies like the European Union, Japan, Australia, New Zealand, the United Kingdom, and Canada had to think twice as to whether US support is really there in case of a military threat, because we have shown in 2021 that we may not be ready to step up to challenge and we are willing to leave chaos and suffering behind us.

That is a giant change in behavior, friends think about it and reflect, and adversaries think of testing the US to see if it's worth taking a risk to get away with a deed of aggression that they perceive to be in their interests.

CHAPTER 21

How do we protect democracy?

The United States has become increasingly divided over time, in part a reflection of imperfect leadership, as under George W. Bush or Barack Obama, or downright poor leadership, under Donald Trump and Joe Biden.

I make no distinction as to party, I'm evaluating our present and past leaders on their ethics, their ability to inspire and unite domestically, to make correct judgments, and to lead our country successfully domestically and internationally.

In the interest of our survival and prosperity, citizens should reflect on the values we have in common, on our points of similarity as a people, on the consciousness among us that we seek to make our country more just, more fair, that we seek greater equality of opportunity and greater equality in how we live – in reality – for all our people.

For the sake of our future we should avoid extreme positions on the left and extreme positions on the right.

Recognize autocratic behavior of the future when you see it, the yearning for power over other people.

When left-leaning Alexandra Ocasio-Cortez attends the super elegant Met Gala in New York City in September 2021 wearing a dress on which is written, stylishly, "Tax the Rich," we need to recognize this behavior as a desire for privilege and a desire for power.

Ocasio-Cortez is the same politician whose influence turned down the establishment of a major Amazon center in New York, which would have created 25,000 jobs. Contrast the two deeds, wearing a costly dress on which were written the words "Tax the Rich" and her opposition to the establishment of Amazon in New York, an important driver of prosperity, and see that the winner was the politician in Ocasio-Cortez. The losers were the 25,000 people who would have gotten jobs from Amazon but did not when Ocasio-Cortes fought Amazon coming to New York.

CHAPTER 21

When Donald Trump contests the 2020 election that was properly conducted, for which votes were tallied in fifty states by conscientious local election boards, his anger and manufactured objection encouraged an attack on the United States Capitol on January 6, 2021. Recognize what it is: unleashed politics at work and a search for power through lies and illegitimacy.

Contrast the fever of the moment on January 6, 2021, with the reality that many of those arrested now have regrets and understand that their behavior was wrong. The participants pay the price, not those that encouraged them.

Recognize that leaders of groups that promote separate identity by gender, by sexual orientation, by color, by extreme political views, "liberal" or right wing, by religion are often power seekers that aim to segment the country for their own personal benefit.

There is no salvation in being divided; strength is in unity.

Appreciate the many beliefs and values we have in common among the 330 million of us. Cherish the sane center of this country, whether you are a Democrat or a Republican. The center of the country is the key to survival, to acceptance of each other of all religions and races and color and of all walks of life, to building bridges to those with different views, to internal compromise, and to set the stage to moving ahead as a unified nation.

Internationally we face a wake-up call: "strongmen" rulers like Vladimir Putin, Xi Jinping, Nicolas Maduro of Venezuela, Viktor Orban of Hungary, Aleksander Lukashenko of Belarus, Narendra Modi of India, Jair Bolsonaro of Brazil, Min Aung Hlaing of Myanmar, whether of the extreme left or the extreme right, are growing in number.

Wherever there are "strongmen," there are divisions, winners and losers. The strongman phenomenon is spreading. All the strongmen have a point in common: rule of their countries by themselves and by their immediate clique. Some of them were elected, some were not, but if elected, they use their power to stay in control.

Ideology is a passing tool to seduce simple and dependent minds, of lesser importance compared to strongman control over politics and the military and determination to rule permanently. The position of "strongman" has its risks: Abdul Karim Kassem and Saddam Hussein of Iraq, Muammar Qaddafi of Libya, Nicolae Ceausescu of Romania, Benito Mussolini, and Fulgencio Batista of Cuba were all assassinated or died on the run.

Many countries in Africa and Central Asia and Latin America have not sided with Ukraine following the invasion February 24 by Russia. There are reasons for this: one is that many are themselves ruled by smaller local versions of the "strongmen" and have personal ambitions to enrich themselves and stay in power forever; another is that many of them are dependent on financial largesse or investments from Russia or China, and they do not want to offend their benefactors.

Along with one-person rule goes privilege for the very few in the inner circle, called "oligarchs" in Russia, money and good living for those, always by unfair and corrupt means, intolerance of minority groups like the Rohingya and the Karen in Myanmar, prison and torture for citizens who object or dissent, and in many cases (China a notable exception), condemning society to slow growth, a poor standard of living dependent on government handouts. Whatever the "strongman" needs to do to stay in power and benefit himself is done.

Despite our deficiencies, the imperfect democracies of Europe, Australasia, Latin America, and North America are vastly better off with freedom, the rule of law, and equality before the law. There may be inequality in our democratic societies, but the inequalities in democracies are vastly less, inconsequential, compared with the inequalities in "strongmen" societies where the very few in the inner circle enjoy all the privileges and vast riches. Among the "strongmen" societies China is the one that, up to now, has given the best opportunities to its own people.

We should not admire these "strongmen" or seek to enjoy their favor.

With some exceptions they have the ability to work segments of the population up into an emotional lather, which is their tool for seizing power. Once that has happened the loss of freedom, the ability to think and act for oneself, the ability to dissent, the possibility to make a good life for one's family are all curtailed in sacrifice to the authoritarian regime. The enthusiasm is wild, but temporary, and the loss that follows is permanent.

CHAPTER 21

To protect our country, its future, and a secure environment for the future of our children, we need to understand how precious liberty is, how much "life, liberty and the pursuit of happiness" means. The people in Ukraine being attacked by Russia do not enjoy "life, liberty and the pursuit of happiness"; they are being killed, maimed, and raped. For their part, the people of Russia, even though most may still approve of Putin since he launched the attack on Ukraine February 24, do not have the right to dissent. They have been told, "if you dissent we will kill you now."

If the United States remains competitive among the nations of the world that will go a long way towards protecting our country. Competitiveness includes having a strong military that is ready to implement *Pax Americana* and enforce liberty and freedom around the world.

Join with our allies who have similar aspirations for peace, honoring of borders and international agreements, and want a good future for their children. That means Europe, Australasia, Japan, China, and Taiwan, and most countries of Central Asia, and many in the Middle East, Africa, and Latin America.

Live and practice and defend values of freedom, fairness, and liberty and be an example that others want to follow. If we Americans do that together in unity, freedom and liberty will always have a home in the United States and in like-minded countries throughout the world.

CHAPTER 22

The task at home ahead for survival and salvation

At every level, we Americans have to start listening to each other.

At work, in social settings, in families, at church and synagogue and mosque, in school we have to open our minds to the views and to the concerns of others.

We have to value our personal freedom and we have to know and practice respect for others in our daily lives, in our thinking, in working. We have to realize that we have common interests, that "the other guy," "the other woman," "the other kid" has a right to live his or her way in freedom without harming other people.

We should never think of taking away rights that people have already gained; we should make certain that people know how precious the rights of freedom and liberty are, to defend them and to enjoy them together.

High among our values and practices must be "first, do no harm."

If you are a politician, a church leader, a civil servant, or a teacher, a businessperson or a union leader or a researcher, don't force people to think your way; be positive, avoid restrictions in thought and celebrate diversity.

The more diverse society is, the better things go.

We need to elect people to our Congress and our administration who will make good, experienced, truthful and ethical leaders for our nation. Test your opinion of candidates for office by asking yourself if the people you vote for are ones that you would like as examples for your own children.

Internationally, our allies matter. Our culture should appreciate the excellent ties we have with other nations; we must keep the channels open, increase dialogue, find commonality, value long associations with freedom-loving nations and peoples, take their interests into consideration, be dependable, and treat every nation with respect.

If we appease strongmen, as Donald Trump did, there will be consequences when the strongmen's adversary nations probe for weakness.

Our behavior in Afghanistan in July and August 2021 was an encouragement to Putin to attack Ukraine in February 2022. Why? Because his reasonable calculation was that the United States was so ready to pull back from international commitments that it pulled out, pêle-mêle, from Afghanistan that it had supported and financed for twenty years.

The problem started with the surrender of its nuclear weapons by Ukraine in 1994 in return for security guarantees, by the Russian attack on Georgia in 2008, and on the seizure by Russia of Crimea in 2014.

In 1994 Ukraine joined the Nuclear Non-Proliferation Treaty and Russia, Britain, and the United States provided Ukraine with security assurances in consideration of its giving up nuclear weapons. France and China joined the agreement the following year. Russia as a signatory violated its word by invading Ukraine, and in terms of the Non-Proliferation Treaty China was wrong to stand silently by and not object in 2022.

The West as a whole exhibited weak leadership vis-à-vis Russia, hoping that the problem of Russia's violations of frontiers was a temporary and finite one. Our collective behavior in these earlier incidents of 2003 and 2014 was an encouragement to attack Ukraine in 2022 on the assumption that the West would not act decisively. Fortunately that turned out to be wrong. The wake-up call came at last after the attack on Ukraine happened.

CHAPTER 23

China and the United States – our similarities

Chinese people and Americans have gotten along well together. It is no accident that the Cantonese name of the United States is "Mei Kuok," which translates as "beautiful country." The United States has no history of colonialism in China, which western European countries and Japan both have, and which is remembered.

There are traits that Americans and Chinese share: a profound sense of individualism, that the free individual can accomplish much, respect for the air of freedom, and conversely a dislike of social structure that places seen and unseen bonds on people. Historically China had to accept various forms of ruling social structure over the ages but never liked it. Though it became an accepted part of family life, the system inherited from generation to generation was part of the social context and there was no choice.

Chinese feel deeply connected to the family and respect it as a basic social unit, far more than to a town, a county, a region, or even the nation itself. That being said, patriotism is increasing as Chinese become prosperous and see the success of their country and growing gain in prestige.

Chinese feel a profound sense of being Chinese, that being Chinese is different, and being Chinese includes a diaspora of overseas Chinese that feels connected, that often does business together, socializes together, intermarries, at times even without the Chinese language in common. For traditional Chinese, race matters at the base.

While individual Chinese and individual Americans have many resemblances, those resemblances stop when it comes to the level of the nation. As nations China and the United States are as different as it is possible to be.

I will put forward a proposition that, I believe, many readers will find surprising.

Understanding and acceptance of our points in common can help China and the United States grow closer, a matter of the greatest importance to the future of both peoples and to all of humanity.

CHAPTER 23

China has 4,000 years of recorded history behind it, yet it thinks of itself as a young country and behaves like a young country. The United States at this writing has less than 250 years of history as a nation: chronologically it is a young country, yet it thinks and behaves like an old country.

Take China first: always based on its culture and its history, it acquired tremendous vigor by casting aside the imperial system in 1912 and becoming a republic. That led to immediate challenges from European and Japanese vested interests in the country and ultimately by annexation of parts of China by Japan and invasion in 1937.

From 1912 to 1949 the Chinese republicans and Chinese Communists fought for dominance. The Communists won in 1949 and took over all of the country except Taiwan, to which the Nationalists retreated, and Tibet and Mongolia which over time Communist China sought to transform into something approaching their own likeness. The victory of Communism gave China a tremendous shot in the arm, leading at times to great mistakes, to suffering, to famine, to redemption but ultimately to a vigorous country with a growing sense of itself as a nation.

The unification and rise of the Chinese nation is a monumental achievement that deserves admiration. With this social change came great economic progress.

China is dynamic, inventive, growing, expanding outward. For the first time in history China overcame natural barriers to communication and travel and created a remarkable network of rail, road, and air connections. Each part of China knows what is going on in the other parts. Modern Internet technology, virtual private networks, and the highly developed surveillance system make it impossible for one part of the country to break out of the nation.

With vigor and perseverance China has insisted on the adoption of Mandarin, the national language, and has simplified the written language from about 12,000 Chinese characters to around 3,000 to 4,000. Those are phenomenal achievements in pulling a people and diverse regions, each with its dialect, together.

China is developing important technology of its own, no doubt in part seeded by discoveries and in some cases intellectual theft from the West, but the

CHAPTER 23

furtherance of technology and its application in practice has led to enormous wealth for hundreds of Chinese entrepreneurs and a vast increase in living standards in China. Technology is put to use in supervising the population; that is easy for people in the West to criticize as an encroachment on freedom, but put yourself in the situation of China for a moment.

The population of China is around 1.4 billion people; that is more than four times the population of the United States. China is ruled from the top, and if one accepts that premise there needs to be a way of keeping track of people, especially when they consist of many different racial minorities within China, each with its own history and cultural traditions going back centuries, many dialects, and several religions. That requires systems to keep track of people and, at least broadly, their activities.

The leadership of China feels that it is "on a roll," to use an American expression, since the death of Mao Zedong and the rule of Teng Hsiao-p'ing. The economy expanded, capitalism flourished in practice under what was nominally a Communist system, while actual Communism, with its poverty, its privilege, and its deep unfairness ended with the demise of Mao Zedong. Since then China has been a model of economic expansion, to the great benefit of the Chinese people.

In the past year and a half, the regime of Xi Jinping has cut some of the most prominent entrepreneurs and aspiring power seekers down to size; that has had a negative effect on growth, but this has yet to play out. Any slowdown in the growth of China will not last more than a couple of years.

China has global geopolitical ambitions: the Belt and Road Initiative seeks to extend Chinese influence, power, trade, and opportunity across Asia into Europe and Africa. Those in need of funding that are less than creditworthy, and government officials in recipient countries may in some cases have taken bribes that they should not have.

The effects are starting to show with pushback from countries that are not happy with the Chinese projects they accepted, with a sense that they have given up control of their destiny to China and inability to service loans. The Belt and Road Initiative has yet to play out, and this will likely turn sour in countries that want to keep their destinies in their own hands.

Add to technology and investment abroad and trade the segment of Chinese military and naval power. In July 2021 China fired, flew, and landed the world's first hypersonic missile. Not only did the United States not possess a comparable missile, but it did not even detect the flight of the Chinese missile.

So, ask ourselves, who is ahead in the weapons game? Is it the United States, or at least selectively, China? The Chinese navy is now the world's largest navy, quietly eclipsing the United States, so smoothly that no one even noticed.

A French newspaper in 2021 picked up on the fact that China has now ordered all ships entering the South China Sea to turn off their automatic locator devices, helpful to know where a ship is in case of disaster, and making it easy to follow the progress of cargo, when a ship is expected in port to pick up goods or to discharge them.

If locator devices are turned off, how is it possible to identify ships and tell one from another? It becomes impossible, short of visual confirmation and direct radio connection between vessel and shore. On the other hand, it would be possible, in the absence of locater identification, to assemble a flotilla of hundreds of Chinese naval vessels around Taiwan, accompany that with an air blockade, and then strangle Taiwan economically without shots being fired or any defender able to do much about it.

Its vigor, dynamism, large and hardworking population, and its optimism in the face of difficulties is what makes China a young country.

CHAPTER 24

How should countries live?

Each country should live its own way, the product of its own history, education, experience, and culture. A country should not have its social organization or a form of government imposed from outside its borders.

It follows that there should not be colonial rule by an outside country, there should not be occupation of one country by another, and going one step farther people should refrain from making moral judgments about the social organization of another country.

We Americans have a growing habit of commenting on human rights in other countries. When we learn about something that doesn't meet our standards we are vocal about it. We single out China because of China's effort to introduce Han Chinese culture forcibly to Tibet and because of the reeducation of its Muslim Uyghur people in Xinjiang.

Many countries are comprised of people of a variety of religious and racial and tribal backgrounds. The origins of such differences are sometimes recent but more typically go back centuries or millennia. Sometimes there are dominant groups and subordinate groups within a country, as was the case with the tribal background to differences between Hutus and Tutsis in Rwanda. Much as Russia seeks to overlook it, there are subordinate groups in Russia itself.

In Iraq under Saddam a 20 percent Sunni minority held power over the Shia majority, as well as over Kurds and Christians. In eastern European countries there were long-standing minorities of Jews and of Roma, traditional nomadic itinerants, and in the Balkans there are Muslims, Eastern Orthodox and Roman Catholic Christians living together, which has at times resulted in civil war.

In former colonial countries like France, the Netherlands, and the United Kingdom, migrants from former colonies became significant minorities. In some countries, as in Syria when it was stable before the Arab Spring, all religions got along well together, Shia, Sunnis, Jews, Christians, all felt at home in Syria and with each other.

CHAPTER 24

These situations are part of the makeup and the inherited history of a country, and may work well or may be unfair to one group or another, and may or may not be oppressive.

How people live in other countries is their business; it is not our business.

Our government should not discuss the internal affairs of other countries with their leaders or ambassadors; we should not make judgments on other countries or try to bring about changes in other countries.

As citizens we Americans have our own views about human rights, reflective of what we regard as basic rights in our own country. Our views about our own rights often extend to judgments about other countries and other peoples, typically without the benefit of knowledge of the history and culture of other countries, in brief, how those countries came to be who they are, their culture, and their history.

Those other countries are not our country.

When we make judgments about them, we overlook that we are not in the situation of those people and those countries, we do not have the historical and cultural backdrop that they have, and we do not live there ourselves.

American judgments on how other countries should live are seen as high-handed and uninformed and are likely to make the air between us and other countries toxic.

In some instances we go as far as sanctioning countries for internal behavior we do not approve of, yet it is largely out of our power to change things in other countries. That is how it should be. Would we like others telling the United States how to live?

Governments in other countries take charge of things in their own way: in a democracy, the people rule; in a quasi democracy, the rulers hold elections and stay in charge irrespective of the results, as with Alexander Lukashenko in Belarus, and in an outright autocracy, those in power stay in power, as with Kim Jong-Un in North Korea.

We are not going to change that, although once in a while, autocrats are overthrown as happened in 1953 in Iran when the USA and Britain conspired to overthrow Prime Minister Mohammed Mossadeq, the 1973 overthrow of Salvador Allende in Chile, and Libya under Muammar Qaddafi. Factions inside do most and sometimes all of the overthrowing, though the CIA acted in the overthrow of Mossadeq in Iran and Allende in Chile. Memories in other countries may be longer than our own, and the 1953 overthrow of Mossadeq in Iran still contributes to Iran's distrust of the USA, seventy years later.

Long-standing distrust, especially if it included overthrow of a regime, makes it difficult to have a civil relationship and to reach agreements together.

The Soviet Union controlled all of eastern Europe and central Asia, forcing communism on cultures with traditions of freedom, and had the ambition of turning every part of the world communist and into ideological allies. It was the worst case of cultural imperialism in recent centuries. The Soviet Union was the ultimate and greatest violator of the policy of noninterference that I recommend.

Although the United States is guilty of relatively few cases of interference in the affairs of other countries, in setting ourselves up as the moral arbiter of human rights, as to what is right and what is not, we expose ourselves to the charge of hypocrisy.

Adversaries we accuse of violations of human rights turn around and point to allegations of mistreatment of Blacks, Native Americans, and Latinos inside the United States and of human suffering and chaos at our southern border with Mexico.

A charge by the United States against China about the treatment of China's Uyghur population ends up with a countercharge against us, greatly worsened by setting ourselves up as the self-appointed arbiter of human rights around the world.

We need to stop being judgmental about other countries and how they run their lives. We all share this world together, and we have to get along well enough with other countries to have pragmatic dialogues and solve external, intercountry issues that arise.

If we are on good speaking terms we can cooperate to save countries and people from disease, reduce the chance of war, take steps to increase trade and prosperity, and reduce poverty for less advantaged countries.

Lower the decibels in our accusations about human rights in other countries, and tone down these highly emotive topics from the discourse between the United States and other countries.

We are not going to change other countries, and in the meantime, we have external and global issues to discuss together with other countries that require a civil and constructive climate.

When change towards greater democracy and improved human rights come to countries where both are in need of improvement, they come through the education of members of their own societies who have been educated in countries where human rights are respected.

Foreign students and businesspeople return home from university in the United States, England and France and Australia and other democratic countries and have ambitions to see the same climate of freedom and human rights in their own countries.

When people choose their own government, the result is usually largely reflective of the culture of that people. That is no guarantee that the government of the people will be a good government by Western democratic standards, but it will be locally chosen and reflect local politicians and culture. It may result in a dictator such as Hugo Chavez or Daniel Ortega, or a popular choice that over time attempts to reverse the political culture of a country like Donald Trump or Recip Tayyip Erdogan of Turkey.

There are times when we should support the powers in charge of a country, even though they may not seem to meet American standards of morality.

Some dictators are worse than others. Bashar al-Assad inherited the mantle of power in Syria from his father Hafez al-Assad, who ruled from 1971 to 2000. Bashar was trained as an ophthalmologist in London before returning to Syria in 1994 after the accidental death of his older brother Rifai, who was intended by his father Hafez to take power.

Bashar did a reasonable job of opening Syria to business opportunities, raising the standard of living and improving security and equality in society. Many émigré Syrians returned after the assumption of power by Bashar to set up businesses and raise their families. Higher education developed and flourished. Though Bashar was not a model ruler according to our thinking in the United States, he deserved our support.

When the Arab Spring came about in 2009, we in the United States did not support Bashar, who felt isolated and behaved with great harshness, torture and imprisonment, towards his own people if he suspected disloyalty brought about by the Arab Spring.

That resulted in an exodus of over two million Syrians from their own country, refugees moving into Turkey and Europe as well as the killing of up to 600,000 people, support by Russia and its army instead of by the United States, and by Russia's proxy Iran.

We in the United States have a part in this debacle. Had we supported Bashar al-Assad in 2011 chances are high that Syria would have remained acceptably tranquil, there would have been no exodus of refugees, no killing of hundreds of thousands of people.

American influence would have remained paramount, Russia and Iran would not have been invited in, and Russia would not have obtained its first naval port on the Mediterranean Sea at Tartus in Syria.

Had Bashar behaved presidentially instead of with weakness and repression in the face of the Arab Spring, backed by the United States which had its embassy in Damascus, Bashar would have likely become the acknowledged leader of the Arab world.

Quite a list of failures, largely avoidable by thinking ahead.

Today the United States is truly out of Syria, an important loss in a critical region of the world. To the surprise of many, Israel always had good working relations with the Assad regime and it is noteworthy that there was never a single border incident for thirty years between Israel and Syria, despite Israel occupying Syrian land on the Golan Heights.

Nowadays things are different: Israel stays in touch with Russia to make certain that Russia does not challenge Israeli warplanes over Syria, there to attack the Iranian proxies Hezbollah, whose attacks Russia is willing to permit despite Iran being an ally of Russia. In Syria, Russia and Iran are competitors. Who would have thought such things possible?

The world is a complicated place.

Except for a fraction of activists, Iranians did not ask for the revolution that put Ayatollah Ruhollah Khomeini in power in 1979, people did not ask for murderous Hun Sen in Cambodia, Vladimir Lenin in Russia in 1917, or Saddam Hussein in Iraq. They did vote for Adolf Hitler in Germany in 1933, they did vote for Benito Mussolini in Italy in 1924, in elections where voter intimidation played a big role.

Autocrats are the product of their times, the politics, the economics, the emotional resentments that grew out of wars. Once in power they stay in power, because they personally control the power, and their taste for power grows with time. Add to the lust for power is the risk that if deposed, a strongman's life will be imperiled as Benito Mussolini was.

For powerful leaders who seize power, there will be enemies waiting to depose them and take power themselves as in the case of Muammar Qaddafi of Libya, Hosni Mubarak of Egypt, and Evo Morales of Bolivia. As an autocrat, one has natural enemies biding their time, and if enemies have the organization to depose a leader they will do so when they feel confident. The coup attempt against Hitler in 1944 failed and the plotters were executed. Some coups succeed, and some don't.

Democracies are better, because their structure contains the means for expression of popular will and thus for change of persons in legislatures and in power. Genuine democracies cannot be imposed from the outside, but democracies can be hijacked as was done by Adolf Hitler in 1933 and Hugo Chavez in Venezuela, as a democratically elected leader turns into an autocrat. Until that autocrat is removed, typically by a coup or a war rather than an election, the citizenry has to live with it.

CHAPTER 24

The world is far from having democracies in all the countries where people would like to have them. Change for the better is in their own hands, and with education and prosperity, the chances of democracies increase.

Change to democracy in countries ruled by autocrats will take time, but it will happen. It is in the hands of the people themselves.

Part V
Four pillars –
a new approach
to the future

CHAPTER 25

List and description of the four pillars

Two achievements are indispensable to the future of the United States: an end to divisiveness, and permanent friendship and peace with China.

The description of the four pillars that follows addresses these two essential needs.

The world we live in is filled with contradictions.

One of my direct reports in business envied me my higher rank in the company hierarchy, and this was his reason: it was clarity that he sought. He used to say that at his level things were difficult to understand but at my senior level I was above the clouds and everything became clear.

In reality the opposite is true. Things become more complex the farther one goes up the power chain of business and of politics. The higher one goes, the more factors and contradictions must be taken into consideration, the desires and vested interests and likely reactions of many people in many countries matter.

Everything gets more complicated.

The willingness to accept and deal with complexity, to overcome the issues and emerge with workable solutions for today and for the years ahead and to come up with clear solutions and implement them is the pinnacle of leadership.

Nothing is easy.

These are four essential pillars to a secure future for the United States and for our people and each of them is filled with challenges and contradictions. Achieving them is necessary but will not be easy and will not be simple.

The four pillars are briefly summarized as **unity**, ending division and getting our social house in order; **economic strength**, ongoing prosperity for our nation and for our people; **defense**, the ability to protect ourselves and our interests against attack, and **friendship and permanent peace with China**.

CHAPTER 25

Unity of the American people is the key to the strength of our nation and is the first pillar. When we are unified, we can act together with insight and understanding to promote the strength and endurance of our nation.

Unity of purpose creates a secure context for our citizens, where we feel that our interests are common ones, that we look out for each other and for the nation.

The opposite, disunity, a problem at present, creates insecurity and dangerous divisions inside the nation. For rivals in other nations, our present disunity creates opportunity for further division through fake news and threats and for attacks on the nation and on our allies.

Economic strength, the second pillar, is the way to build strength and prosperity in the nation at home, satisfaction with lifestyle starting with the basic needs of food, shelter, and clothing and moving forward on traditional American middle-class affluence. Economic strength builds security for individuals and for families, opportunities for betterment, a future for young people, and reasonable satisfaction with status in every walk of life.

An important part of economic strength is acceptable economic equality, especially equality of opportunity to enjoy freedom of kind of work, of employment, and sufficient economic means to build a good life.

Economic opportunity must be the same for all at the starting line, irrespective of gender, race, religion, color, sexual orientation, and physical handicap; no one should ever be held back because of inherent prejudice or discrimination. Merit, good ethics, and work must be the criteria that count.

Defense is the third pillar. Having had a position at the top of the world's military power pyramid since World War II and having had the benefit of *Pax Americana* since 1945, and managing to avoid nuclear war since 1945, we need to keep a preeminent position. Our military must be strong and capable of successfully taking on any aggressor against the United States, which does indeed have a global role in peace. It has been a good thing to be the world's policeman; where we have created problems was by starting avoidable wars ourselves.

The fourth pillar is **friendship and permanent peace with China**. We have to do it differently from what we do today, which is largely reactive, reflective of our long-standing desire for the status quo.

I recommend a new approach, **a treaty of friendship and permanent peace with China**, requiring an innovative mindset, imagination, and understanding of risk and opportunity both from the United States and from China.

My proposed fourth pillar is more important and farther reaching than the original courageous approach out to Mao Zedong by President Nixon and Secretary of State Kissinger in 1972. It is a global agreement with China, a way of getting along together for the foreseeable future.

Pillar four is novel and included in Part VI of this book, with individual chapters in what should be in an overarching understanding and treaty between China and the United States.

In the next chapters I describe steps needed to make these four pillars reality.

The needed ingredients are there in the American people, our history and our culture, and the potential power of our economy and our military. What has staggeringly hindered a move towards each of these needed pillars is highly divisive politics, biased media, fake news, unstated but implied acceptance of inevitability of decline, lack of proactive thought about the future, and poor, at times chaotic, leadership.

We need better leadership in Congress as well as in the presidency, and the election of capable, ethical, unbiased officials who will be examples we are willing as a nation to follow. For friendship and permanent peace with China, the subject of pillar four, we need to be unified and we need visionary, honest, and courageous leadership.

There is no doubt that we Americans are up to the challenge if we are willing. Like everything worth doing, it's up to us.

CHAPTER 26

We have to get our house in order
"United we stand, divided we fall"

This is the most difficult part of this book to write, because there is no obvious solution to unifying our country.

Our country is a family of citizens, with common interests together, a shared situation in the world, and a future together, but at present our nation is deeply divided.

Internal divisions cause weakness and ineffectiveness, dislike among people inside the country, and unpredictability and distrust of the United States by other nations.

As a nation we have been exposed to extreme people on the left, extreme people on the right, fake news, conspiracy theories, all of which have been damaging.

Citizens have a critical role in electing people to office who are unifiers, not dividers, who understand the importance of the nation coming together.

Start with oneself

Unity starts at home, in our daily lives, in our connections with other people.

You and I and each one of us has mental and social conditioning, which is the result of early upbringing, of family influences, or experiences at school and at work.

We may not be able to change who we are but we can become tolerant of others, understanding of other people's views, and sympathetic to their needs. We can build bridges to people of different backgrounds, different political views, and different objectives.

We can listen to them, and they can listen to us.

Recognize where you and I may have adopted, or gone along with, extreme positions that do neither us nor our country any good, and to the extent that extreme positions inspire suspicion and dislike of others, do our country and ourselves harm.

Middle of the road, calm and collected, views and actions and activities are what we need to unify our country around the great majority of society that hopes for a safe present, a secure future for ourselves and our children, a prosperous nation at peace, universally liked and respected, a traditional example of liberty and freedom for others.

Middle of the road does not imply weakness: it reflects an understanding of the greater good for everyone, left, right, and center, nourished by the citizens of our democracy, focusing on the values we share and the needs we have together.

Tolerance of others can take us a long way to unity.

Our future can be bright if we work together, in peace and prosperity, and make it so.

Openness and truth and understanding that we are all in life together encourages schools where cooperation and understanding and consideration for others is learned. If teachers and parents think that way, growing children will too. Children are naturally ready to learn from older people, so when children are taught kindness and understanding, tolerance and outreach to others, they are likely to grow up that way.

Group sports in schools and community events are a builder of understanding and cooperation, tolerance, respect, and friendship for others.

Faith in the integrity of our voting

In the United States voting is organized and supervised at the level of the community and at the level of the state. People who give their time to administer voting in elections are people interested in serving their communities, their states, and the nation.

They come to that important work with a commitment of evenhandedness, to run elections openly and honestly, "let the chips fall where they may," and report results of how people have voted whether or not results agree with their personal preferences.

CHAPTER 26

These people are performing a voluntary role as citizens. Their personal views have no part in the administration of elections, and the people who do this know that. They deserve our thanks and our trust.

Security and safety for all of us

To be unified we need safety and security for all of our people. "Law and order" may have a pejorative tone to some, but law and order is what we all want. The most disadvantaged people are the most exposed to crime; they are the most in need of a safe environment in which to live.

What enters the head of the rare policeman or policewoman who shoots a victim when that could have been avoided? Is it bad training, fascination with the power of weaponry, a misplaced sense of superiority over others? Power-hungry support groups, media, and troublemakers contribute to the idea of unfairness by the police, the rage for justice, and in every case, divisiveness.

There have been horrendous, murderous, completely unfair departures from the proper role of police with the loss of innocent lives.

Changing attitudes of some, though not all, of our police forces is a big job. That needs to be done in some communities and locations but not in others where the situation is satisfactory. It is a task that falls to communities and states, as many of the truly important tasks do. Being a police officer may imperil the officer's own life: his or her willingness to take on a job that may be dangerous deserves our thanks and respect.

In the interests of the security of everyone, all 330 million of us Americans need to welcome police in our communities. But that welcome must be based on the certainty that a police officer will not do anything unjust that harms innocent people and that persons suspected of crimes will be treated as human beings, with observance of the law and presumption of innocence.

Deserved confidence and trust in the police is a contributor to the unity we need.

CHAPTER 26

Internet and social media and their role in divisiveness

The Internet and social media have an enormous influence on our lives; we are only at the beginning of this and how this plays out will be seen in the years ahead.

Children are exposed to computers and smartphones from an early age; working on a computer or a smartphone as compared to in-person learning, games, or conversation is distancing oneself from others.

It is important for parents and families and schools to realize that distancing happens. As such, we need to place limits on social media exposure and to make sure that the youngster is fully integrated into family life, into school life, into sports, and into society.

Just as we used to place limits on children watching television, now we place limits on being on the computer and on the smartphone. There are serious risks in becoming alienated in the world of social media, including bullying young people, fake news intended to make us believe and behave in directed ways, predators, and the naive belief that real life is not with other people but on the Internet and on social media.

With excessive exposure to the Internet the risk of alienation, dissatisfaction with oneself and with life, depression and suicide becomes higher. The Internet should be a tool and not become our master. Living life on the Internet and in social media contributes to divisiveness and harms unity, as it is not a connection with real people.

At its worst the Internet and the "dark Internet" merchandise pornography and are home to extreme political views, factionalism, and conspiracy theories that may seek to take down our government and way of life.

When that happens to young people and to adults who are easily influenced by and susceptible to emotions and causes it is the very opposite of the engagement, stability, and common sense that we need as individuals and that our communities and our country need to encourage and support unity.

We need to understand the potential of the Internet for influencing people, even you and me. Keep your distance, test everything you see on the Internet for its veracity and how it looks when you apply common sense. Real life, work together, learning together, living and sharing in a community, and using the Internet as a tool and not as master of our emotions helps build our sanity and our unity.

Working in a place of work or working from home
The effect on unity and disunity

The coincidence of Covid and new technology possibilities in 2020 created the need to avoid exposure to others with Covid. This allowed the concurrent opportunity, through emails and virtual private networks, for some kinds of work to be done from a remote location.

Work from a remote location did not apply to jobs held by service people like cooks, waiters, bus and train drivers, taxi drivers, police officers in squad cars, firemen and garbage collectors, border patrol officers, as well as to people who manufactured things such as the foods we eat, including meats like chicken and cattle and steers, which need to be slaughtered and cut up into portions.

Quietly a new class distinction emerged in society, workers who had to be in person on the job, and those whose work and connected electronics enabled them to work from home. Workers on the job in person were more likely to be exposed to Covid, which caused the near collapse of some businesses, like restaurants, and shortages of meat.

Class distinctions are inherently divisive, but the phenomenon of being able to work from home for some or not being able to work from home for others created a new source of divisiveness.

The freedom offered to some by electronically aided work is only at the beginning and has a long way to play out.

Persons working from home have better command of their time. They may work for their company a full eight or ten or twelve hours as required or they may decide to work less than agreed, thus surreptitiously depriving their employer of owed time.

Working full-time at home may allow time for a doctor visit or an essential errand to pick up children from school. Benefits of working from home can include looking after children, cooking and cleaning, and playing computer games.

The vast majority of people who work from home are likely to be conscientious and honorable and not take advantage of it. Others may not be, trolling the Internet during work time, appearing at work Zoom meetings with the video turned off, thus concealing that they may not have shaved, showered, dressed, that they are trading on their personal computer in crypto-currencies, or that they are in bed.

"Working from home" is a contribution to divisiveness, as the work team members are not in personal touch with each other in a company office, thus do not have the benefit of being in direct contact with their peers, bosses, and reports.

Candidates applying for jobs that can be done remotely may insist that the job require their presence physically at work only two or three days a week or possibly not require their physical presence at work at all. If the company doesn't meet the demands of the employee, the employee will not accept the job.

A job with these concessions, that the employee only has to appear a few days a week or possibly not at all, may seem attractive to start with, but is it in the long-term interests of the new employee, herself or himself? The absence of human contact, of having to cooperate in person, work through conflicts, likes and dislikes among people is a great loss, because interaction among people is what humanity is about. Without it, we miss it, and we do not know what the effect of missing it will be. Certainly it is diminished engagement and likely diminished responsibility, accountability, and trust.

A friend of mine has a son who has an analyst job with a bank; the father recommends to his son that he go to work in person, that he actually get to know his colleagues, and that he work with them, thus being in direct touch with other people and developing teamwork. The son answers that he can get more done faster working from home, and that he thus saves the time and hassle of commuting to work. My friend worries that that is all good, but how will he learn how to work with other people?

CHAPTER 26

Bringing people physically into the work place promotes teamwork, understanding, engagement, commitment, and confidence.

We have not yet mastered the psychological and social effects of "working from home" but this trend weakens our ties to each other, our sense of community and our unity.

Unifying our country in this time of disunity is critical. A sense of community, working for the common good, engagement with others in family, in school, in sport, and at work, and especially nowadays – engagement in person, promotes understanding of the other fellow, the other woman, growing confidence and unity.

Summary of the need for unity – what can we do?

In unity we are strong and remain an example of freedom and decency for the rest of the world, the destination of choice. Prejudice, hatred of others, jealousy, and conspiracy theories have no place in good government, which is what we must have.

Vote for people who favor high standards of children's education everywhere, making certain that disadvantaged areas enjoy top-quality results-based schooling, that youngsters are held to the same high standards everywhere, and that we encourage the next generation to improve their global competitiveness in learning and to aim high.

Vote for people who think of the country as a whole, all 330 million of us and counting, who have a worldview and a future view and who understand that the United States cannot fall behind among nations in the economic race or in military capability.

Which is more important and more threatening? To argue about unborn fetuses, or to avoid annihilation by an adversary with nuclear and biological and cyber weapons?

We need better leadership than we have had in recent years, new leadership that understands the enormous risk of a divided people and the external threats we face.

CHAPTER 26

On the side of restoring unity in our country is the passage of time. As the expression goes, "time heals all ills," and our divisiveness is a great ill. With the passage of time the pendulum will swing from disunity to unity.

That will help, but we need national unity much earlier than what the passage of time may bring us. Read the newspapers, watch news in the media: we face serious, and growing, outside threats that could have serious consequences for the United States.

Don't wait for time to unify us or for an adversary to force unity upon us too late.

As you go to the polls in November, whether you are Democrat or Republican or independent, put the nation and all its citizens including its young people ahead of party loyalty. Vote for leaders who think of all of our people, of all of the complicated and at times conflicting interests of our country, and who can restore unity to the nation.

CHAPTER 27

The economy we need

We require a prosperous, globally competitive, American economy.

We Americans have a great culture for a prosperous economy, and that culture of work and creativity continues to be there, alive and well. Resourcefulness was a quality essential to survival for the original settlers of this continent, and equally, it was required of the immigrants that came to the United States and who continue to arrive today.

Resourcefulness is the mother of invention and the mother of hard work in getting things done. Along with resourcefulness is the knowledge that how we do is up to us as individuals. Despite some of our politicians working to create a feeling of dependency in exchange for votes, we Americans have an inborn sense there is no government that will provide, that it is up to each of us to strive and succeed and to provide for our families and to give them the basis for a good future.

Along with these qualities is the feeling deep in many immigrant Americans, that while they individually had to undergo uncertainty and labor-intensive work for small pay and little rest when they arrived in the country, in the air of freedom of the United States their children might have a good future, college educations, better jobs, security for themselves and their families.

In thinking like this we are very Chinese, and when Chinese think like this, they are very American.

Immigrants are an enormous source of strength for this country, new people, an incoming leaven to shake up older attitudes, usually with a foreign language and different ways of working, ready to do the hard work that some are not prepared to do.

Once immigrants become citizens and have a sense of ownership and belonging in the country; they vote. The vote matters to them as individuals, decision-making about what is now their own country and what kind of leadership they want.

With freedom, immigrants think for themselves. They do not need to be given a group identity and led to polling places; they know what is good for them and what is not. Contrary to what some people think, immigrants are not in the United States because of welfare handouts; they are here for safety and work and opportunity for the future.

Throughout the history of the United States, immigrants have contributed to our economy and our society, and that continues to be true today. Immigrants contribute, they do not diminish, whether they are or were English, German, Italian, Polish, Russian, Haitian, Mexican, Central American, Afghan, Iranian, or Ukrainian. They all have contributed and new immigrants attempting to cross the border, legally or illegally, soon contribute too.

That the United States is still a magnet for immigrants, the most desirable country for immigrants on earth, is a tremendous source of strength for our country. It is a counterweight to the aging of the population, to its becoming ingrown, to a potential lack of fresh ideas, and to misplaced satisfaction with always doing things the same way.

If we had to buy this attraction of immigrants to the United States, we could not possibly buy it; it is priceless. Long may it endure.

Good schools for all citizens, especially the historically and presently disadvantaged, high standards of achievement, and the zeal to learn, greatly improved from the present, will keep the United States in the top economic rank of nations.

Good education for all is the single most important factor in having a competitive economy. We need to spend our education income at the state level, not at the federal level, to ensure that there are good public schools, junior high schools, and high schools. Standards for achievement should be high, not artificially depressed in the mistaken belief that we will help minorities by lowering standards.

We will not help people by lowering standards. It is high standards, and the same standards for everyone, that foster the equality at the starting line that our people need. Private schools, charter schools, and religious denomination schools must be available as a choice for parents and children and as a yardstick against which to measure student performance. If public schools are performing well, the results of the students should be available for all to see; if one kind of school is doing better, or worse, the public should be aware of the results, to press the underperforming one to improve.

The federal role in education should be to update standards and publicize how we are doing as a nation. Are we moving up from the low position of thirty among the world's nations in how our young people are doing in math, reading, and science? Our objective should be to be among the top ten nations of the world in the ranking of our students in the next five years. If we do this, our future as a prosperous and successful nation will be greatly enhanced.

This will do more for us than financial giveaways for votes, and more than weaponry.

Business innovators must be encouraged to start, to take risks, to develop, and established businesses should be encouraged for the employment they create and their contribution to the economy.

People who start businesses are unsung heroes: they put their well-being and their money at risk. If they fail, they have lost their time and their money; maybe they have outstanding debts. If they succeed, they are on a path to create employment for others, stability for themselves, and a good example for those who don't have the ideas or willpower to start or who are burdened by existing commitments.

The United States should become a tax-friendly location for business and individuals, instead of being one of the highest taxed countries, which we are today. Business is drawn to establishing in those countries where the tax take percentage is reasonable, and if we combine reasonable taxation with good laws and justice for all, freedom and lack of prejudice and personal liberty, we have an unbeatable combination.

Every one of us needs to realize that we live in a competitive world, that training and development of people as well as investment in the best software and hardware boosts our productivity; boosting our productivity is the key to reducing inequality.

Some politicians reinforce the idea of inequality emotionally by saying that there are insiders who benefit and outsiders who are deprived. In reality, most income tax is paid by well-off people: 38.8 percent of income tax is paid by the top 1 percent of earners, 59.4 percent of income tax is paid by the top 5 percent of earners. Loopholes allowing super rich to escape paying tax get much political play, are destructive to our country, and should be closed.

A step that would reinforce the ownership of every citizen of our country is for every earner, regardless of economic level, to complete and file an annual federal tax return, and to pay a minimum federal tax of $100 each year.

A payment of $100 federal tax a year is affordable for everyone. It would give a sense of ownership in the country to low-income taxpayers; it would be a modest contribution to the services and benefits received today and to the Social Security the taxpayer will receive or may already be receiving.

When people own something, they value it and take care of it.

Our citizens must take ownership of our country, and a minimum annual tax payment by each citizen will help, even if he or she receives far larger federal benefits than the $100 he or she is paying. Every person paying tax has a stake in our country and tax thus binds us together and helps create ownership and a strong economy.

Wherever possible, government spending other than defense and services for the entire population should be at the community level, at the local level, and at the state level rather than the federal level.

Communities are like households: they understand their needs best, they know better what to spend on and what to avoid, and once spent, they will keep track of the expenditure and the results.

The farther away from the citizenry that spending takes place, the more likely it is to be politically motivated, offering opportunities for personal power of politicians rather than results for the citizenry. Citizens are entitled to oversight over government income and expenditure, and spending in Washington, D.C., is extremely difficult to control as it is likely to be opaque. It is not easy to compare the income of a government department with the services it renders and with its overall benefit for the citizenry.

Communities should make discussion of their income and their expense part of the public dialogue, just as some families do. From teenage years on, young people should know how their community gets its income and how it spends its money, how much is left over, or the amount of deficit and how that is financed. When a major project comes along that needs financing beyond normal income, such as building a school or a bridge, residents should be part of the dialogue, their representatives should be part of the decision. By discussing these things openly, residents take ownership and help build our economy. Not everyone will agree on every decision, but the dialogue and the majority vote makes everyone an active participant, and even those opposed take a degree of ownership.

Dialogue about government income and expense builds transparency and builds leadership, both qualities greatly needed, and that root out suspicion of what is going on and at worst, the fear of conspiracies. Let everyone who is interested in government income and expense see everything and take ownership.

The same is true at the state level and even at the federal level. Interest in how our states and how our federal government finance themselves, their income and their expenditure, should be a community discussion matter, and citizens should make their views known to their congressmen and senators.

The combination of federal and state taxes should create an atmosphere of inquiry, or discussion, and understanding among taxpayers that they are getting value for their money at the community, state, and federal level. Conviction that we understand our government income and expense, and that we are getting value for it, will make our country stronger in that by knowing the facts, we emphasize our ownership, and by emphasizing our ownership, we will take better care of what we own: our country.

A controversial topic that has so far been dealt with emotionally, not factually, is the benefit – or otherwise – of globalization of trade. We are now in a mode of thinking that the United States has overdone it. That is, that other countries have benefited from globalization at the expense of the United States, that we have been the losers in the globalization of trade, and that it is time to pull manufacturing back into the United States.

This is a tough issue, with arguments on both sides of the question. In my mind, globalization of trade has been mostly, not entirely, to the benefit of the United States and very much to the benefit of the standard of living of people in countries that have founded new industries and exported their production to other nations.

From the standpoint of humanity as a whole: globalization has greatly raised the standard of living, brought more people into the middle class, improved healthcare and availability of water and electricity and the Internet to literally billions of people who were able to undertake manufacturing for which there was a demand. For the family of humankind, the six billion of us, globalization has been beneficial, and that matters.

For consumers, the ability to obtain products at lower cost than in their home country, through economies of scale and through lower wages, has been of immense benefit. Were it not for globalization, we in the United States would be driving more expensive, more primitive motor cars that would use more fossil fuels and do more polluting. We would not have jet airplanes for our vacation and business travel, as the parts for a single jet airliner are put together by manufacturers in multiple countries. We would not have the variety of foods, the array and range of clothing at reasonable prices, the countless building parts starting with steel and lumber and copper that come from other countries, and the engaging foods imported from other countries.

Left to our domestic resources alone, we Americans would have an economic existence that would cost much more, give us far less choice, and a problem of shortages requiring people to plan their purchases ahead, take time to shop so as to make sure one doesn't get left out, and lead to hoarding of items.

Where globalization has hurt the United States is primarily in two areas: 1) It has led to abandonment of certain kinds of manufactures, which could be made cheaper, and often better, in other countries. Abandonment has led to loss of jobs and, far more insidiously, a loss of skills not easily replicated. Electronics has further contributed to the loss of manufacturing skills, as increasingly workers seek to work from home. 2) Some industries have substantially disappeared from the United States, like the clothing industry, which inevitably has gone to countries where there are large numbers of workers available to make clothing inexpensively.

At present we are in the mode of "reshoring" manufacturing to the United States, and a further refinement, "friendshoring" manufacturing to countries that are allies of the United States. If "friendshoring" becomes a requirement, this will become a huge opportunity for mischief and corruption, all of which adds to cost and which will be very inflationary.

"Reshoring" of manufactures that have long since been made in other parts of the world will not work; on a major scale, it will result in massive losses and disappointment as to availability and quality. The abilities to make some things in the United States have been lost over the years; the skills would have to be rebuilt, plus the facilities to manufacture would have to be rebuilt to the standards of 2022 and years ahead.

The costs, including of training, higher material costs due to onshore sourcing, trial and error, are likely to end us up with products that are far more expensive but inferior in appearance and in performance: the American buyer will not be happy, and the exercise of "onshoring" will have cost the United States big money.

What is the solution to the globalization dilemma? Back to education! We need to educate our young people to be globally competitive, with abilities and work ethic as good as a Japanese or a Chinese or a Korean. We have to do what we are best at, high-efficiency manufacturing where computers replace human beings, for products with very high value added, and design of new products and new processes, where we put our imaginative and creative genius and resourcefulness to work, where we are ahead of other nations and stay ahead in our inventiveness of products that perform better and use less energy, less of the earth's resources, pollute less, and give total satisfaction.

That is where our economy has to be. Good national leadership will understand it and get us as a nation thinking and acting creatively in the best interests of the American market and thus of ourselves as citizens. We cannot turn back to the past in manufacturing; there is no salvation there, there are only missteps and losses.

CHAPTER 27

While we are improving our education and energizing our country, practice globalization, have the benefit from globalization work through to the American people as well as to the people of other countries. Globalization makes everyone better off.

CHAPTER 28

Cutting-edge military with undisputed technology

Democracies are special in that the military is subject to civilian rule, a great strength, and a quality that enables citizens to sleep peacefully at night, knowing that there is a citizen in control. There has been no attempt since 1776 to upset the civilian government by the military; the military is trained to understand that the civilian government, in the person of the president of the United States, is in charge.

It is a universal recognition that despite the troops and the weapons at the disposal of the military, they serve the nation, thus they are always under civilian control.

The president has the power to declare war if he should so decide and the president is responsible to the people, so he or she takes care in committing US military force. Once committed, the US military has a remarkable track record of doing an excellent job of peacekeeping, of fighting, always under ultimate control of politicians.

It is at that point that things become difficult: President Donald Trump had admiration for autocrats like Kim Jong-Un and Vladimir Putin, thus our national interests took a back seat to his personal likes and dislikes, and President Joe Biden seems intimidated by Vladimir Putin's threats, thus pays attention to his warnings.

The personalities and preferences of American presidents become our national policies; the actions of these individual leaders are minutely parsed by adversaries to gauge the future reaction of the United States to their planned activities when these conflict with American interests. That conflict of interest happens often in many parts of the world.

The policy of deciding to commit, or not commit, the US military is the single most important decision that a US president must take, including the awesome decision of the "finger on the button" of launching a nuclear war.

CHAPTER 28

As a general comment, the United States president should threaten less and keep his policy options to himself. However, when he does threaten, including by "drawing a red line," he has to act in accordance with that threat and what could happen.

If he does not act on a "red line," the subject of a threat, the United States has lost status, that is, it demonstrated that it doesn't really mean what it threatened. That is a wide-open invitation to adversaries to take aggressive action, seeing that the United States has not acted, that it proved, to use the time-honored expression, "to be a paper tiger."

Our chaotic withdrawal from Afghanistan in August 2021 and abandonment of the country and its people to the Taliban was a clear sign that the United States had no taste for international engagements; there is no question but that the rushed and disorganized withdrawal from Afghanistan contributed greatly to Putin's decision to invade Ukraine, a mere six months later.

Had the United States and allies, and a modest force from the United Nations, remained in Afghanistan, it would have made our twenty-year-long commitment to Afghanistan and its people worthwhile, and chances are very high that the Russian invasion of Ukraine would never have happened.

The important lesson is that giving in to little threats because of fear of consequences, and ducking out ignominiously from a serious international commitment like Afghanistan, carries a heavy price of a larger aggression later, once an adversary has taken the measure of the will and commitment of the United States president.

To threaten and not act is extremely dangerous, because it may lead to aggressions by adversaries that really must be countered, at much higher risk because more is at stake. President Biden has now said three times that the United States will defend Taiwan against attack by China, which considers Taiwan as part of China. Under the circumstances of President Biden's words, the United States must now defend Taiwan if attacked, with the involvement of US military and naval forces.

CHAPTER 28

Should the US bring back the draft?

As always, people are everything.

Men and women who join the military clearly want to be in it and view the military as an opportunity to learn, to test their physical and mental capacities, to experience teamwork in pursuit of an objective, and possibly to advance in the military itself as a career. For those who are drawn to it, it is a great way to live, to advance, and to make friends.

There has been no draft since 1973.

Reintroducing a universal draft, now in which every man and every woman reaching the age of eighteen would serve in a branch of the US military for two years, will be the least liked part of my recommendations for the unity of our nation.

However, a draft would have enormous benefits: it would increase the size of our military, put more trained young people in uniform, greatly increase the abilities and teamwork capacity of young people, and provide a larger universe of persons to draw on for promotion and leadership. Very important: a draft of men and women would be a further big step in promoting even more equality of men and women, serving to launch more women in the higher-grade capabilities that our modern economy needs.

Our excellent military colleges, West Point, Annapolis, the Coast Guard Academy, and the Air Force Academy, are globally admired and have exchange students from foreign countries.

Our military has to be the best in the world, cutting-edge technologically, so as to be the first line of defense, unassailable, for the United States and for all allied countries that love freedom and liberty. Our military needs to be prepared for the wars of the past, the present, and the future.

Why the past? An adversary may use tactics of another age because that is what he knows best. In February this year, Russia attacked Ukraine from the north with a column of tanks and vehicles forty kilometers long. These proved easy pickings for Ukrainian anti-tank weapons, and the Russian attack on Kiev failed. France prepared for World War II by constructing the Maginot Line, which would have served France well in World War I but was easily bypassed by the German army in World War II.

Preparing for many different kinds of war is demanding. Afghanistan was a war against guerrilla units that attacked at unexpected times and places. Assuring freedom of navigation may take more than traditional aircraft carriers, it may require a twenty-first-century version of the PT boat made famous by World War II such as Iran now uses in the Arabian Gulf, and it may take many such boats supported by nuclear submarines and drones. Hypersonic missiles have to be made, better than those that China already has and Russia claims to have, and effective defenses against them developed.

Outer space is likely to become a war zone with aggressors' satellites directing hits, deflecting our missiles, and dispatching cyber weapons. Some fighting is likely to be partly unmanned but vastly more destructive to military in the field and to civilian populations.

With increasing numbers of countries possessing nuclear bombs, the temptation to use them will increase, not least since they have not been used against people since 1945. Unprecedented attacks may take place with cyber, chemical, and biological weapons. We have to be prepared for everything, and we have to be the best.

The United States has to spend big money on weapons development, testing, and on the training of people to operate them. Money spent on the military, including on an expanded military through a draft, will be money well spent. It will be a positive message to allied countries that cherish their freedom and a strong message to potential adversaries that the United States is serious about protecting its interests.

Our position in warfare has to be such that no country will ever attack the United States or its allies. We and allies will be safe because any aggressor will understand that if we are attacked, nothing will be left of them. Vladimir Putin conveys this same message, but in the case of United States weaponry, it is actually true.

It has to stay that way.

CHAPTER 28

Refraining from criticism about human rights in other countries is entirely separate from aggressive behavior from other countries that are threatening to the United States and its allies. Not only must we be completely free to address aggressions, but at some times we will have to do more than complain about behavior and impose sanctions. Military action will be needed in worst-case scenarios and when that happens, we have to act decisively, without threats and without warning.

Part VI
A new relationship between the United States and China

CHAPTER 29

Treaty of friendship and permanent peace

The nostalgic ambitions of Russia, the desire to have the world on its own terms, the lack of forward-looking leadership in the United States, and the subsidiary and yet very considerable ambitions of North Korea and Iran have led to political posturing, the invasion of Ukraine by Russia, and ongoing threats and counterthreats.

Through Russia's unprovoked actions the war in Ukraine became a reality, with consequences for Russia itself and countries that depend on Russian gas. The end result is unknown, but that this is an ongoing reality, costly in Russian and in Ukrainian lives, in property and enormous economic damage, is a fact.

Potentially more important with far-reaching effect would be clashes between China and the United States. Imprecise consciousness of the coming rivalry between China and the United States led to the "pivot to Asia" during the Obama administration. The next steps and outcomes of potential clashes are unknown, but they can easily result in hostilities.

China's fortification of the nine dash line that includes sea routes to Japan and Korea as well as geography claimed by other countries, Vietnam, the Philippines, and Malaysia is a permanent, ongoing source of conflict. A constant risk is China's reminder that Taiwan is, in its view, cemented as part of China, and that it will be reunited with the mainland, and Joe Biden's statement on three occasions that the United States will defend Taiwan. That explicit policy statement has dangerous potential consequences.

The liberal way of a democracy including that of the United States is to prefer a quiet life and to leave things internationally as they are. American passivity and disengagement in recent years has led to global loss of status, declining influence, replacement of the United States by Russia, by China, in regions and forums where we did not expect it. Neglect of relationships with our allies in key regions has led, and is leading, to problems the outcome of which, left to themselves, is not known.

Neglect and misunderstanding characterize our policies and effective withdrawal from the Middle East and the "pivot to Asia." From the most important foreign country in the Middle East region at the beginning of this century, the United States has now become a minor player in a critically important part of the world. Even worse, at the same time it has unintentionally advanced the status of Iran as a potential adversary. The administration of each president from George W. Bush on played a part in this unnecessary and costly decline.

At a time when the United States is divided and focused on internal issues, the world has become an increasingly dangerous place. Nine nations of many different political persuasions, many ruled by "strongmen" like Xi Jinping, Vladimir Putin, and Kim Jon-Un, and some, like Pakistan, with a government and society in turmoil, possess nuclear weapons and the missiles to launch them. These countries and others possess devastating biological and chemical weapons and secretive and surprising cyber weapons, undeclared and unknown until they are used.

As we Americans bring our own house in order and unify our country, there is an international task to be done. We need excellent and dependable relations with allies, countries that think the way we do and with whom we share common interests.

Equally we need a strong initiative to arrest accidental slide into ever greater distrust and hostilities between China, and its ally Russia, and the United States and the West. There are increasing points of international conflict with potential for incidents, for unexpected surprises that can rapidly spin out of control.

The tone of language between China and Russia and the West has greatly deteriorated, and language should be read as what is going on in the minds of rulers and of nations. The chance of an accident, leading to hostilities, has increased.

The visit of Nancy Pelosi to Taiwan in 2022 was, in the Chinese view, a provocation, and it was answered by the largest ever Chinese military exercises using live ammunition, missiles, and aircraft as well as naval vessels on four sides of the island of Taiwan. As I write today, two US navy ships are sailing through the Taiwan straits, which are in the global view international waters but in the view of China, domestic waters between two parts of China, the mainland and Taiwan.

Following the Pelosi visit, China deliberately cut back its relations with the United States to eliminate direct discussions on military matters and on climate. When communication channels are removed, risks arise from lack of normal access and absence of pathways for exchange of information.

The United States, Japan, and European countries like France and Britain and the Netherlands have sent their naval vessels through the Taiwan straits. Not only do they have the right to do so, but they are demonstrating to the world the right of free passage through waters that are critical for access to and from Japan and Korea.

What would happen next if a US navy or allied ship hit a mine during their passage through the Taiwan strait today? It could lead to hostilities.

There are those who think that if there were hostilities over Taiwan, war could be contained to a region, such as the air over Taiwan or the water around Taiwan. But history repeatedly demonstrates that is not true.

A setback in defense of the island by Taiwan, or a setback in attacking the island by China, could in either instance lead to broadening a war, attacking of each other's naval vessels, attacking military sites in China or on Pacific islands, or even as a major escalation, use of nuclear weapons.

When something in war goes wrong, what happens next is unpredictable.

At present we are running dangerous risks. These must be put under control for the sake of our two nations and of humanity. A new approach to international issues is needed.

The need for a new China–United States relationship

For the future of the world, the United States needs a special relationship between China and the United States, based on acknowledged mutual interests, negotiated together in understanding and friendship and cemented in a permanent treaty together.

CHAPTER 29

A firm relationship of friendship and permanent peace, enshrined in a treaty between China and the United States, will be an invitation for other countries to join in.

A proposed new relationship and treaty between the United States and China is described and discussed in the chapters that follow.

For a negotiation of such an important treaty, one which fundamentally can influence the future of humanity to the better, China and the United States must come to such discussions as clear-eyed equals, each from a position of strength.

The military power and potential of both China and the United States have to be convincing, likely different in objectives and scope and reach, but comparable in potency.

The economies of the two countries have each to be of critical importance to them, and the more dependent the Chinese and American economies are on each other, the better.

Each country of China and the United States has to feel strong for this to have a chance for this relationship to be conceived and to work.

For a treaty to be negotiated and signed, it must have the support of the overwhelming majority of both lawmakers and of the population in both China and the United States.

In the case of the United States, this is where unity of our country, the principal requirement conveyed in Parts III, IV, and V of this book, is so important. The United States will never be able to agree on a treaty as vital as that of friendship and permanent peace with China unless it feels strong, master of its own fate, and unified.

The essential unity and strength of the United States will be illustrated by the approval by two-thirds of the US Senate of a treaty with China.

For China the political process is simpler, as political power is concentrated at the top. That pinnacle may nonetheless disguise different currents of opinion at the level below leadership of the country. It is critical that such an important initiative on the side of China be greatly supported by the vast majority of the Chinese population, who must see it as being in their interest and to their benefit and prestigious for China.

In the United States objections to such a treaty would be vociferous; in China, dissent may be less noisy but under the radar screen. A treaty that is seen as disadvantageous to the United States will never be ratified by the Senate.

Dissent in China could be dangerous to a treaty that was not well liked by the broad Chinese population. In taking the temperature of the people, China must listen to popular views just as much as a democracy as the United States does. People of both countries have to agree and support what is going on in their political administrations in agreeing to a treaty of friendship and peace between the two countries.

CHAPTER 30

Turning a new page

China and the United States need to turn a page, and form a new relationship, based on understanding of the risks of behaving as China and the United States each do now. We need a recognition of how much we two countries have in common, a determination to be friends and act as friends, to avoid war between them forever, and to be partners in the peacekeeping of the world and a benefit to other nations.

Implicit in a new relationship is recognition that the United States and China are militarily and economically strong and that their people are in favor of friendship and peace between the two countries. We need to understand that in the twenty-first century, they are the leading powers in the world and that their cooperation together is essential for their own future as well as for the survival of mankind.

The concept of this new relationship must capture the imagination of the leaders of China and of the United States. Time is of the essence. There is no time to lose. Both countries are running big risks at present, which has the possibility to sour relations further and, in the worst case, to lead to armed hostilities.

Looking at such a treaty from the standpoint of opportunity, a treaty would lead to very substantial growth of both the United States and Chinese economies, including reduced inflation, improvement in the standard of living, and the chance to address global economic and climate and social problems together. Each nation would know it has nothing to fear from the other.

The concept of a new relationship has to be agreed soon between Xi Jinping and Joe Biden. The two leaders are scheduled to meet at the Bali, Indonesia, meeting of the Group of 20 nations on November 15 and 16, 2022. If that is too soon, it should be done in the first half of 2023.

Joe Biden needs to stand back from day-to-day political concerns and take a broad and deep view. He needs to imagine the huge benefit to the United

CHAPTER 30

States and the remarkable legacy his administration would leave to the United States if this can get done.

Xi Jinping may find it relatively easier. He has shown a strong sense of direction, broad and deep, and a remarkable grasp of world affairs that is in substantial part due to his own thought.

The United States in the person of Antony Blinken should reach out to Wang Yi, foreign minister of China, to say that the United States is working on a treaty of friendship and permanent peace between China and the United States. This should be done in advance of an in-person meeting between Joe Biden and Xi Jinping.

The Group of 20 should be the forum in which this treaty of friendship and peace is conceived. That has several advantages: the Group of 20 would be "in at the birth" and would implicitly have a role of supporting and encouraging China and the United States to move to a treaty.

Member countries of the Group of 20 are Argentina, Australia, Brazil, Canada, China, France, Germany, India, Indonesia, Italy, Japan, Republic of Korea, Mexico, Russia, Saudi Arabia, South Africa, Turkey, the United Kingdom, the United States, and the European Union.

Conclusion of a treaty between China and the United States would be of immense benefit to all nations, as the world would become more secure, a safer place to live, more prosperous economically, and would encourage work together on sustainability problems like inequality, water shortage, pollution, and global warming. It is not too much to say that for most countries the conclusion of such a treaty would be "a sigh of relief."

It would be a big step forward in the advance of civilization, away from hostilities and enmity, towards international cooperation. A by-product would be a great increase in prosperity over time for less advantaged countries, more people enjoying the benefits of a middle-class living standard, and a better future for young people.

The question may be asked, why not conceive and build a United States–China relationship through the United Nations?

It would not work.

The United Nations suffers from the structure established in 1945 at the end of World War II, which specified that the five Allied Powers that prevailed in World War II (the United States, Britain, France, the Soviet Union, and China) each had a veto power in the Security Council. That has chronically hamstrung the United Nations as members of the Security Council, including the United States, have exercised the veto when it suited their own interests.

The membership of the Security Council has changed character. The Nationalist China regime, the member when the UN was established, fled to Taiwan and their seat was taken over by the People's Republic of China in 1949. The Soviet Union broke up in 1989 and was replaced by Russia.

The United Nations organization structure is rigid and not suitable to top-level conversations on the future of mankind. It is also highly politicized and said to be corrupt in how influence is traded among countries and blocs within the United Nations in awarding key jobs within the organization.

Member countries take predictable and ossified sides based on the pattern of behavior and the evolving political lineup of the past seventy-seven years.

The United Nations is not the answer, and the future of the United Nations is limited and uncertain. Just as happened to the League of Nations, established in 1919 after the First World War, the United Nations has partially outlived its usefulness, and if a United States–China friendship and permanent peace treaty is agreed and enacted, the UN will most likely lose its usefulness.

Work between China and the United States in the coming months between now and mid-2023 should be on broad lines and principles and the outline of a treaty document should be drafted. The concept should include ideas from both China and the United States, elements that benefit both countries, that will ultimately require to be approved in both countries.

CHAPTER 30

The most important single point is an agreement that China and the United States bind themselves to an agreement of friendship and permanent peace, of avoidance of war and hostilities. If ongoing circumstances affecting one or the other of our countries, China or the United States, raise the chance of hostilities, the two countries will discuss the issue together under the treaty terms and resolve it without hostilities.

If this idea captures the imagination of Xi Jinping and of Joe Biden, working on such a treaty will take time, at least six months until key elements are in place and agreed together. That Xi Jinping is likely to be reelected as secretary of the Communist Party for a third term is highly positive, as it will add a vital element of stability from the Chinese side. Joe Biden will have two more years to serve as president, less stability in time than that of Xi Jinping, but sufficient time to complete a treaty.

In the United States the treaty would have to be approved by a two-thirds positive vote in the Senate. For this to happen, it is absolutely essential that both Democrats and Republicans sign on to the enormous value of the proposed treaty. If that happens, it will not matter, from the standpoint of the treaty, which party controls the Senate, as it will be a bipartisan effort in the interests of the nation. Everyone will get credit for it.

Ideally, the treaty will be ready for approval by both governments by mid-2023. Xi Jinping should have been reelected to a third term in November 2022, and the United States Congress will have been in place six months after midterm elections on November 8, 2022, and taking office January 3, 2023.

There should be a working group office established with a high-ranking and experienced team of Chinese and a team of American civil servants, working together in a place distant from their capitals, Beijing and Washington, but convenient and reachable. Hong Kong could be a good choice. The teams would report jointly to the foreign minister of China and the secretary of state of the United States.

English and Chinese would be the working languages. All work would be shared and transparent; problems would be identified early and resolved. The treaty itself would be written in Mandarin Chinese and in English, each version to be identical in every detail and each version to be binding on signatories.

During the time the treaty is being worked by the China and United States working group, there should be meetings between the foreign minister of China and the US secretary of state every three months.

The first quarterly meeting should immediately follow the November 15, 2022, meeting of the two presidents and should establish and staff the working group and provide an early sense of direction. The next meeting in February 2023 would examine and review the accomplishments of the working group so far and would give direction for the work required during the coming three months.

The next meeting in May 2023 should have shortened and refined the issues in preparation for a concluding meeting at the end of June 2023. By that time all parts of the treaty should have been approved by both the Chinese and the US administration, keeping all parties informed throughout the process, so that approval is completed as expected and later ratification by the US Senate takes place without a hitch.

During the seven months that the treaty is being negotiated there should be a mutually satisfactory stand-still agreement written by the foreign ministries of both countries. This should be implemented right after the November 15 meeting between Xi Jinping and Joe Biden, refraining from all acts of any kind by either the United States or China that could be perceived as hostile by the other country.

Acts in the stand-still agreement would be specifically listed, to include absence of military maneuvers by either country in the South China Sea, no additional arming of Taiwan, no additional arming of man-made islands inside the Nine Dash Line, no propaganda by each nation against the other, no fake news, no cyber warfare or sovereign-sponsored hacking, no espionage by either country, no new tariffs or artificial impediments to commerce, no complaints to international organizations by either about the other, no harassment of visitors or businesses in either country.

All stand-still agreement topics should be covered in further detail and agreed in the permanent treaty. At the time of signing of the treaty, the Friendship and Permanent Peace Treaty replaces the stand-still agreement.

CHAPTER 30

After the treaty has been signed and ratified, the working group between China and the United States would become a permanent secretariat to deal exclusively with the treaty, its implementation, and issues that arise.

The smaller the permanent secretariat is, the more weight it will carry with the signatories. If it is possible to keep it to twelve people from the Chinese side and twelve from the American side, consisting of two senior ministers and ten sector specialists from each side, it will do a workmanlike job.

CHAPTER 31

Recasting the job of world policeman

Critical to the future of the both the United States and China is the agreement in the treaty that military activities of the two countries are never undertaken as adversaries, but in concert, for the security of each of them and for the entire world.

The task undertaken by the United States as sole world policeman since the end of World War II has over time led to disagreements, inability to enforce good behavior, and has contributed to aggressive behavior between China and the USA, Russia and the USA, as well as North Korea and Iran.

The reality of the United States as the sole world policeman is outworn. Events have led to a change of view as to the willingness and dependability of the United States to carry out this activity. Failure to enforce red lines under the Obama administration, the cultivation of strongmen and distancing from allies under the Trump administration, and the disastrous American withdrawal from Afghanistan under the Biden administration all contributed to the erosion of the view that America was a dependable global policeman.

The dynamic growth of China, its economy as well its military and naval reach, and the nostalgia of Russia under Putin in seeking to re-create the territorial reach of the Soviet Union have likewise contributed to eroding the image and the reality of the United States position as global policeman.

The job of global policeman has to be done in a new way.

It should be shared equally between China and the United States as part of the Treaty of Friendship and Permanent Peace.

The basis for performing that task must be a mutual understanding and agreement between China and the United States of the concept of sovereign stability in and among nations and what that means in concept as well as in practice. Agreement between China and the United States leads to discussion and agreement to what constitutes an incident requiring the two countries to do their job of joint world policemen, how the policing will be undertaken, how the risks will be shared, and the desired outcome.

To do that job effectively together is enormously worthwhile for the world and a great contributor to stability. It is a complicated job requiring trust, to be implemented for cross-border issues involving land or sea borders or airspace or outer space issues as well as massive movements of people and threats of hostilities involving countries.

The job of global policemen should not normally extend to domestic issues inside a country, but there may be exceptions to be agreed upon together between China and the United States. Examples would have been the Bosnia civil war of the 1990s, where external players contributed to inflame a country with religious divisions, or the oppression and expulsion from Myanmar of the Rohingya.

An even more sensitive issue like the invasion of Ukraine by Russia on February 24, 2022, will have to be addressed with understanding and firmness, as Russia considers Ukraine part of Russia and Ukraine considers itself an independent country, recognized as such internationally.

For long-standing cultural, historical, and geographical reasons each of China and the United States has a sphere of influence in its region: in the case of China, Southeast Asia, and in the case of the United States, the Western Hemisphere.

Neither China nor the United States should set up any new military or naval establishments in the sphere of influence of the other without the concurrence and support of the other. Rights of free passage for all countries in international waters and skies should be guaranteed for all trade and noncriminal passage by China and the United States.

Each of China and the United States has primary responsibility for keeping the peace in its sphere of influence. Each should inform the other when it is concerned about threatening activities from third countries within each of their spheres of influence, when joint action may be needed and how it may be undertaken.

The actual enforcement of keeping the peace should be done jointly by the United States and China together, their military and naval and space and cyber defenses working in concert, including addressing jointly on the ground, at sea, and in the air aggressions that take place within their own sphere of influence. Working together to keep the peace will give the military of China and the United States familiarity with each other, satisfaction in the task they are doing together, and growing comfort level.

Other countries may be interested in joining the peacekeeping effort, which should be welcomed and encouraged by both China and the United States.

That China and the United States, as the two leading global powers, will do the global policemen job together will help to deter adversaries, so there are likely to be fewer disturbances of international peace. There is less chance that countries will try to play off one against the other, as China and the United States will be a common front.

The basis for the treaty is openness and candor between China and the United States leading to confidence and to the most priceless of all qualities in relationships, trust.

Viewed from the perspective of other countries, including Russia, a critical aspect of the treaty is how effectively China and the United States share the task of world policeman and how well they trust each other. The world will be watching. The working group set up by China and the United States will include the two most senior military and naval officers from each country, implementing the stand-still agreement and working towards completion of the treaty.

During the process of sharing the job of global policeman, China and the United States should exchange Information on the scope for reducing armaments of both countries, on a mutually needed and mutually desired basis, while retaining enough weaponry so that China and the United States can together take on the function of global policeman under the treaty without fear of challenge by other countries.

CHAPTER 32

Taiwan

A Treaty of Friendship and Permanent Peace between the United States and China will be more closely vetted and parsed in Taiwan than anywhere else, because Taiwan has potentially the most to gain, or the most to lose, in the text and reality of this treaty. In no country will the treaty be of as much interest as in Taiwan.

It is critically important that Taiwan be consulted and involved from the start. It must feel that the treaty is greatly in its interest, and not to its disadvantage, in order to receive the enthusiastic support of Taiwan.

Taiwan has supporters in the political spectrum of the United States. Those individuals in Congress and in the US administration must know with certainty that the future treaty is in the interest of Taiwan as well as being in the interest of the United States and of China.

In the treaty, the United States recognizes and reiterates the "one China" principle that was agreed to in 1972, which includes the statement that Taiwan is recognized as part of China.

In turn the treaty between China and the United States will assure the people of Taiwan the right to their own government and their way of life, ruled and administered from Taiwan. Taiwan will include in its constitution that it is part of China and renounces in perpetuity any moves or statements that propose to separate it from China.

Over an agreed period of time, say three years, Taiwan will disarm and become a neutral country like Switzerland. Relieved of the tension across the strait from China, Taiwan will become a more important technology and business leader, expanding into other technology fields beyond its present global lead in cutting-edge semiconductors.

Unlike Switzerland, which has its own military, the security of Taiwan will be jointly pledged and guaranteed in perpetuity by the United States and by China.

Trade and investment between China and Taiwan will be publicly and strongly encouraged. Chinese will be encouraged to invest in Taiwan, and the Taiwanese encouraged to invest in China. On both sides, legal and practical rights of investors and traders will be protected in perpetuity.

Economic ties between China and Taiwan are strongly encouraged, deepened, and strengthened, and where feasible, economic progress in each country is designed as complementary to the other, so that economic integration becomes as close between Taiwan and China as they are between China and the United States.

Communications between China and Taiwan will be improved, starting with direct air transport and ferries between Taiwan and China. The feasibility and cost of an undersea rail and road tunnel between China and Taiwan will be evaluated, to result in a fast transport system similar to that under the English Channel between England and France and Belgium.

Critical decisions concerning Taiwan will be guaranteed by China and by the United States and enshrined in the treaty. The level of trust among Taiwan, China, and the United States must be just as supremely high as between China and the United States in the treaty, indeed even more so, as Taiwan has much to lose if the treaty is not meticulously observed.

The treaty section on Taiwan must have the involvement and the agreement of the Taiwanese government and the enthusiastic support of the Taiwanese people.

CHAPTER 33

Economic interdependence of China and the United States

A key section of the treaty will provide for greatly increasing interdependence between the Chinese and American economies to the benefit of both countries.

The economic integration of China and the United States is already the closest in recent history between any two countries. To find any comparable relationship, one would have to go back to the integration of Great Britain and the United States in colonial times and the trade and manufacturing relationship between Great Britain and its colonies, particularly India in the 1800s.

Large, easy-access markets are essential for industries that require efficient, large-scale production inspired by costly research. An exception is niche products for highly segmented markets, where quality and uniqueness come into play rather than quantity. China–United States cooperation is of the large-market type.

What is unique about today's interdependence is the huge size and complexity and endless variety of the Chinese and USA economies, combined with twenty-first-century movement of people by air and gigantic shipments by sea and by air, with universal use of electronics and the cloud for instant communication of data, of information on materials and availability, timing and pricing. Interdependence today is a creature of the twenty-first century and hugely benefits its participants.

The benefits to the United States are that American companies access components and materials and American consumers can buy end products that are varied, high quality, and generally speaking within reach of everyone. The availability of Chinese-made consumer goods is so obvious that Americans never even think about it. Putting it another way, the availability of Chinese manufactures has greatly added to the variety and color of America's lifestyle, at an affordable price.

CHAPTER 33

Referring back to chapter 10, the way the United States pays for its goods from China is on credit by creating more dollars. The price the United States pays for interdependence with China is a loss of jobs to manufacture certain goods, ergo a measured shrinkage of the manufacturing sector, and what is more subtle, a loss of human skills to manufacture goods that are made in China. Something that for the most part remains in the United States and probably increases over time is the design capability of the properties, ingredients, and performance of goods to be made in China.

What China gains from the interdependence of the economies is a vast expansion of its own economy as it has geared up over the decades to serve the vast United States market, for the most part indirectly, as China made goods are branded with American trade names, and Chinese-made components simply vanish into the complexity of the end package.

The gearing up of the Chinese economy has brought hundreds of millions of Chinese people into the middle class, launching Chinese families into major consumers of clothing, building supplies, good housing, food, energy, and hard goods like appliances and especially automobiles. China has become the world's largest market for automobiles, in 2021 there were 21 million cars sold in China despite the restrictions (and at times, chaos) of China's Covid regulations, beating sales of under 15 million in the United States and under 12 million for Europe.

That hundreds of millions in China have joined the middle class and enjoy the benefits of an affluent lifestyle is a source of stability, desire for peace, and for further development, an enormous benefit to the entire world.

The economies of China and the United States are thus deeply connected; the mutual interest of both countries needs to be acknowledged and promoted. How deeply connected China and the United States are is seldom even recognized, especially by American politicians who impose laws and tariffs and regulations without seeing through to the end effect of their actions.

China has over the years become the principal supplier of manufactures to the United States. Most things that America uses in industry and in consumer life have China content. Here are examples: components of aircraft, aircraft engines, parts of motor cars, furniture, electric appliances, wiring and light bulbs, sporting goods and uniforms, tractors and industrial equipment, cosmetics, medicines and pharmaceuticals, building products.

A highly sensitive area up to now has been the Chinese consumption of lithium for electric cars. China consumes 40 percent of the world's production, which comes mainly from Australia, Chile, and China itself. Without lithium it's not possible, at least for the present, to power electric cars. A much less known, but in fact even more sensitive, area is that of rare earths, essential products in cellphones, computers, and weaponry. China controls 80 percent of the global market and has at one time used stoppage of rare earth exports (to Japan, in 2011) as a negotiating tactic. The United States has several projects under way, the most important of which is with Lynas, an Australian company that sits on top of the world's largest rare earths mine in Kalgoorlie.

The key areas of lithium and rare earths can be addressed in the treaty so as to assure a smooth and interruption-free passage of these vital minerals between China and the United States and other countries around the world that need them.

The United States is a major supplier of agricultural products to China, in which the United States competes for market share against Ukraine, Australia, Canada, and Brazil, among other countries. It is a matter of reality that the United States buys far more from China than China buys from the United States; the trade balance is unfavorable to the USA, the shortage being paid for in US dollars, which are added to the currency reserves of China.

Regulatory steps can be taken to improve China's access to the American market: China should be given "most favored nation" status, which facilitates access to Chinese manufactures, and existing quotas on certain Chinese goods should be eliminated.

The United States should cease negative statements about the Uyghurs in China and about Tibet. These are internal Chinese matters where, unlike Taiwan, there is no risk of international conflict. As noted earlier in chapter 24, it is time to stop commenting on and meddling in the affairs of other countries.

Countervailing steps should be agreed to and taken in China to facilitate American access to the China market for products and services, including tariffs and especially artificial trade barriers to American participation in and investment in the Chinese economy. Forced disclosure of technology by American companies to Chinese companies as a price for entering the China market should be stopped and participation in the huge China market made easy without required surrender of information on products and processes.

The United States eliminating harmful and discriminating trade measures on China may result in howls of objection from other countries that have gained for themselves some of the benefit of measures the United States took to contain China.

Such objections will result in overall lowering of manufacturing prices on imports into the United States: other countries will lower their prices, and Chinese exporters will lower prices. Business continues, and the US consumer gains as well.

American investment in China, and Chinese investment in the United States, should be encouraged through the treaty of friendship and peace. Investors prefer certainty, and the treaty will bring about a reassuring investment climate framework that will give confidence to businesspeople in both countries.

The legal and tax framework in both countries should be made understandable so that people feel secure in starting China/US trade, or US/China trade, and investment in each other's country. Both sides should cease threatening sanctions.

Just as it is in a domestic home country situation, people who own something in a country not their own will value it and will seek to preserve it and take care of it. Cross-border travel, and cross-border investment, will benefit the economies of both countries and promote contact between peoples, understanding, and trust.

Tourism is an important factor for the start of deeper interest, and tourism should be made easy by waiver of visa requirement for up to ninety-day stays in each country for passport holders of the other.

Two benefits of having greater China–United States interdependence will be a favorable effect in reducing inflation, compared to the costly and cumbersome "re-shoring" of manufacture to the United States and to the equally costly and contrived "friendshoring," manufacture of goods for the American market in countries that are regarded as "friendly" to the United States, which is likely to be uneconomic and lead to hard feelings if a country is not classified favorably for "friendshoring." Second, greater integration between the Chinese and American economies is likely to perpetuate and expand the acceptability of US dollars in international trade, all financed by borrowing, the subject discussed in chapter 10. Digital currencies in both China and the United States can be discussed together.

Closer economic integration has many benefits for the activities of China and the United States together in the future, such as in space, in undersea exploration and resource development, global control of fisheries and avoidance of overfishing, and joint development of projects in third countries, all activities that will benefit China and the United States as well as all of mankind.

CHAPTER 34

Technology cooperation

The history of technology exchange between China and the United States has not been a happy one.

In the context of a treaty of friendship and permanent peace, technology exchange at the governmental level can make sense if it is on the basis of "mutually needed and mutually desired" sharing, with approval for significant exchange of technologies to be agreed between both countries at the governmental level.

Private corporate interests, in both China and the United States, must be honored and not set aside or disregarded. Dealing with applications for technology exchange and acquisitions of companies in either country that involve technology will be part of the work of the secretariat.

Private business that has mutually attractive market share in view, benefiting Chinese companies and American companies, combined with respect for each other's work is a good way to increase exchange. Companies acting on the basis of profit motive are well qualified to see when exchange will be beneficial, and the two governments can encourage exchange and provide a solid legal framework to protect exchanges.

As friends committed to permanent peace, the exchange of technology between China and the United States is encouraged; areas will be found to deepen interchange, to promote technology sharing in the interest of both China and the United States and the entire world.

Because there will be a path for mutually desired and agreed technology exchange, unauthorized technology theft by either side will be classed as espionage and will be forbidden by the terms of the treaty.

CHAPTER 35

Exchange of information on weaponry

For the treaty to work and serve the global peacekeeping role shared by China and the United States, each of China and the United States, and the two of them together, must have the strongest, most effective, technologically cutting-edge military.

China and the United States will inform each other on development of weaponry and will back their knowledge of each other with a section in the treaty of friendship and peace on weaponry that each holds assurance that it will never be used against the other and openness by both countries to global disarmament in stages, which would be led by the United States and China.

Weaponry should include military hardware as well as cyber and biological and chemical weapons and must cover weaponry and any kind of hostilities in outer space.

Codicils may be added to the treaty on disarmament by kind of weaponry. This should be done by China and the United States in stages at a cadence that ensures that these two nations permanently have the upper hand in weaponry in comparison to third countries with significant military or nuclear, cyber, biological, and chemical weapons.

In their shared role as global policemen, no country should be able to challenge the cutting-edge quality, reach, and performance of weaponry of China and United States.

This is truly an area of enormous potential for mankind. If China and the United States are committed to permanent peace and friendship, it will have the effect of discouraging other, lesser players from starting trouble as they will know that China and the United States will act jointly to stop them.

In turn, when peace prevails and confidence in peace and stability grows around the world there will be increased readiness to disarm, because the policeman task will have been entrusted to China and the United States. A world where there is truly and permanently less spent on armaments will allow resources to be devoted to problems like the environment, global warming, clean air and water, and a decent life for all.

CHAPTER 36

Cooperation on global issues

China and the United States will exchange ideas and cooperate on issues of importance to the entire world to include disarmament, global warming, adequacy of fresh water supplies for all humanity, air and water pollution, equality without distinction as to gender, race, color, and religion, and threats from outside the earth's atmosphere.

Both countries will set an example for leadership and outreach to other global organizations, dedicated to control of global warming. They should closely coordinate their views and standards and work to encourage other nations to join them in these critical tasks.

This is an area with enormous potential for humanity, especially for poorer countries in Southeast Asia, Africa, and Latin America. As peace becomes the expected reality, resources of the United States and China, working together, can be dedicated to infrastructure projects in developing countries, better global healthcare, exploration of outer space and the depths of the oceans.

The purpose of Chinese–American cooperation on global issues will be, to put it simply, a secure and better life for people everywhere.

CHAPTER 37

Associate treaty members

This is an area of challenge as well as opportunity.

It is critical that the concept and the birth of the China-United States friendship and permanent peace treaty originate from the Group of 20. Those are the twenty nations that have the largest populations, the most trade, and the largest economies, so that the Group of 20 is in at the birth and has a connection with it and a share in credit for it.

It is vital that the nations in the Group of 20 see the China-United States treaty of friendship and the permanent avoidance of war to be to the benefit and advantage of their own nations and every nation.

Why is this so?

Friendship and commitment to avoid war gives China and the United States a permanent interest in working together, in sharing information, technology, and coordinating action around the globe.

Each nation in the Group of 20 should be automatically invited to be an associate to the treaty from the beginning.

As other nations subscribe as associates, they would likewise be bound to be included in the friendship and commitment to avoid war.

That said, the work needed to negotiate with and to sign up nations to be associates to the treaty should not be minimized. There will be countries that consider themselves in a special situation by reason of history, of unachieved ambitions, of lack of good relations with their own neighbors, of disputes over natural resources, different political systems, or disputes among the people in their own country.

Every member nation will accept friendship and the avoidance of war as a welcome principle, however nations that have territorial expansion in mind will see joining as an associate in the treaty as a limitation on what they can obtain by guile or by force.

Russia with its territorial ambitions is an example: if Russia emerges with gains from the Ukraine war that it started February 24, 2022, it may think next of joining with Belarus to regain the Baltics or Poland, effectively challenging NATO to attack and do nothing about it. Against a weakened or indecisive NATO, such a bluff may work; in a strong NATO, which is the case now, Russia will suffer reverses and heavy losses.

Russia is a difficult case for two reasons: One, Putin has "painted himself into a corner" as the expression goes, with the invasion of Ukraine, continued threats against other nations and against the West, and the strong and growing array of sanctions against Russia and its key leaders and businesspeople. The invasion, the posturing, the threatening rhetoric all have to play out before a sensible conversation with Russia can start. Two, Russia is the junior partner in the China-Russia relationship; China can keep Russia in mind as discussions and work for friendship and permanent peace between the United States and China begin.

The single most country for which such a commitment as an associate would be binding in practice would be Russia. Territorial ambitions that Russia has would have to be set aside in favor of the commitment to friendship and peace. Therefore, Russia would give up the possibility of territorial aggression on its neighbors, but it would gain the respect of the world and have the opportunity to develop the lives of its people and its economy in permanent peace enforced by the two global policemen, China and the United States. Depending on the point of view of Vladimir Putin, this could be a good arrangement for Russia and a great legacy for Russia under Putin.

The key to the involvement of Russia is China. With the economic weakening that Russia suffered through the Ukraine war, the losses of soldiers and equipment, and the greatly increased dependence on China and India for oil sales, Russia will have little option but to become an associate in the treaty of friendship and peace if China demands it.

The decision of India to join the treaty as an associate would be a great boost to India and a further prod in the direction of Russia for it to join. A great incentive would be that nations that joined as associates would give no cause to be under sanctions, once the past had been settled.

If Russia signed on, and its aggression in Ukraine stopped, its trade and assets should be unfrozen and it should return to a normal position in the society of the world.

Similar arrangements could be imagined with Iran, Myanmar, and North Korea. Once the world's major countries subscribed to the principles and the reality of the China-United States peace and friendship treaty, the advantages of being an associate will be manifest and many countries will want to join.

A difficult case would be Iran, which has an enduring religious rivalry with Sunni-populated countries and has had a signal growth in influence in the Middle East through activities of its armed proxies. Iran would require pressure from Russia to join as an associate, but when it did, this amazing country and people could become part of the global family of nations, trading and developing its economy. The enhanced degree of freedom may not be easy for leaders of Iran to accept, so Iran might remain a holdout, to the great cost of its gifted people.

The European Union, NATO, and the United Kingdom, all significant power brokers in their own right, are likely all to be associates; as experienced nations with very long histories, they will jointly and separately "trust but verify" in the words of Ronald Reagan. Every associate will want to know that the treaty is real, that it is central to the thinking of China and the United States, and that it will be adhered to and beneficial to be an associate.

The presence as associates of Japan and the Republic of Korea, both democracies with a deep culture and heavyweights among democracies, as well as Australia and New Zealand, will be of immense importance, not least that they are allies of each other and of the United States.

In Southeast Asia Indonesia, Malaysia, the Philippines, and Singapore, as well as Thailand and Vietnam, Cambodia and Laos are likely to strongly welcome the treaty as it will add an important measure of stability in their own backyards.

Countries in the Middle East will join if the principal players, China and the United States, lead. That will include Saudi Arabia, the United Arab Emirates, Israel, Egypt, Algeria, and Morocco, and predictably, whoever will control Syria and Libya. African countries will join as there is likely to be great economic benefit in the wake of the treaty. The action of Nigeria in joining will be pivotal as will that of South Africa.

Scarce resources will be able to be devoted to education, health, and economic developments. Increased prosperity will give citizens a greater stake in the game for themselves and their descendants, and the dangerous violent insurgencies that oppress Mali, Somalia, and Niger will gradually atrophy as prosperity increases.

Canada will be a quiet partner at the United States table from the early stages on, just as Russia may be a quiet partner on the China side. Mexico will value peace and the increase in prosperity the treaty will bring; as a major nation it will want to be part of it, as will Latin American countries as a group.

The presence of Argentina and Brazil as associates will be of great importance as other Latin American countries become associates. Joining the treaty as associates may be a highly unifying event in Latin America. For countries in Latin America, the treaty will liberate resources that are today devoted to armaments to be used in the development of their people and their economies. Indirectly the treaty will lead to a better life for people in Latin America.

India will not want to be left out of this. If India joins, Pakistan and Bangladesh are likely to join as well. The contact through the treaty and the joint activity of China and the United States as global policemen may reduce the likelihood of war between India and Pakistan and, as time goes by, assist in the nuclear disarmament of both countries. For Sri Lanka, becoming an associate would give the country status and would help the path back to solvency.

CHAPTER 37

Countries that have ambitions to gain territory or control by invading another country would not be able to join such a treaty, and if they did and broke the terms of their association, they would be subject to joint action by China and the United States, which would share the job of global policeman.

Other associate members to the treaty interested in joining an association led by China and the United States are the British Commonwealth and Switzerland, New Zealand, Australia, and Southeast Asian nations including Indonesia, Thailand, Malaysia, and the Philippines and Papua New Guinea.

The treaty should be so attractive that no one will want to be left out.

CHAPTER 38

Importance of starting now

The most important of all these countries, by far, are China and the United States since we together have the most at risk and, concurrently, the greatest opportunity.

Person-to-person talks give better opportunities for mutual understanding, truthfulness and accountability, and a growing degree of mutual confidence and trust. Everything has to be transparent, needs and desires and concerns, all topics discussed, nothing hidden. If leaders are truthful and transparent, mutual trust should gradually come about.

The key in all of this is that the work should begin now. It needs a thorough understanding of history and cultures, intellectual breadth, vision, and the aptitude to undertake a challenging task. At this point the United States, during both the Trump and the Biden administrations, has developed a rigidity of its own, casting China as the enemy.

For a conversation with China to succeed, this negative bias must be put aside. It will take great minds and a great leader to start such high-level conversations and have a chance at success. Harry Truman, Dwight Eisenhower, Richard Nixon would have been up to the job and in contemporary times, Barack Obama or the late John McCain.

Designating one's opposite number as an adversary will never work in high-level conversations. The top leaders will have to look upon each other as knowledgeable, trustworthy, deserving confidence, and as friends, emblematic of the friendship of their nations.

The timing for starting is good. Moving forward on the treaty will work if China and the United States start talks as equals, understanding that each has enormous economic and military power and that it is in the interest of both to work together.

Until this is started and completed, we live in a perilous world, in which issues have to be dealt with on an individual, tactical basis. The risks, the threats, the recriminations and reprisals and danger of world war will continue until the United States and China determine to talk together, agree together in their own interests on broad policy lines, and become friends dedicated to permanent peace together.

Afterword

If we in the United States do not seize the opportunity to develop and move forward with this proposal, it is likely to be because the book is not widely read and not read by persons in government with influence. Also likely, that the idea is adopted by one political party but not the other and becomes one more pawn in the divisiveness of our country.

It will be difficult to enlist support, get this moving forward inside the government, and get it done. There is every chance that the proposal will be considered too unusual, too extreme, or that some will like it, some not, and that it will get stranded in party politics.

I am known in business and financial circles, less so now that I am eighty-eight years of age, but unknown in politics and only slightly known in literary circles, all of which is a disadvantage when putting forth a new political idea. I understand that.

To address the problem of being unknown as well as the potential partisan problem, I will send a copy to a number of congressman and congresswoman and copies to President Biden and the members of his cabinet, as well as to the members of the Supreme Court. Likewise, I will send it to friends in Hong Kong in the hope that they can get copies into the hands of the leadership in China.

If having become aware of the proposal, and thought about it and discussed it, the United States government still does not move forward, it is likely to be because we do not see enough advantage for the United States in it, or that we think that China could gain an advantage on us.

Also possible is the more unsettling and insecure feeling among our congresspeople and leaders that as a nation in negotiating and signing this treaty, we would not be acting from a position of strength.

Pursuing and concluding this treaty would be an enormous advantage to the United States and to China over time, with immediate short-term benefits but ongoing and far more significant benefits over the medium and long term.

That does not mean that the leaders of the United States and of China will see it that way. China may feel that it is already sufficiently dynamic, on an economic and military "roll," not to need this treaty. The United States may not pursue it because we have become culturally attached to defending the status quo during the past fifty years.

We in the United States may consider that the risks of continuing to act internationally in the present way are acceptable, that things should stay the same, and that we Americans, through our unique position in the world, will manage well enough by following the same path of internal division and ad hoc reaction to external events as they arise.

Do not believe that.

Pursuing the status quo and ad hoc reaction to outside events will not secure our future.

The risks of catastrophe are great. Cooperation, understanding, and friendship and peace are essential, beneficial in reducing the risk of war and making our economies more prosperous, a better place for less advantaged people in many parts of the world.

Let us start on this now. There is a great opportunity ahead.

Bibliography

Orlando Figes, *A People's Tragedy: the Russian Revolution*, Penguin, 1996

Hedrick Smith, *The Russians*, Sphere Books, 1976

Karl Marx and Friederich Engels, *The Communist Manifesto*, Monthly Review, 1964

Pierre Lorrain, *La mysterieuse ascension de Vladimir Poutine*, Rocher, 2000

Leon Trotsky, *Ma Vie*, Gallimard, 1953

Shi Naian, translated by J. H. Jackson, *The Water Margin*, Tuttle, written 1368

Luo Guanzhong, translated by Yu Sumei, The Three Kingdoms; book one *The Sacred Oath*, book two *The Sleeping Dragon*, book three *Welcome the Tiger*, written during lifetime of the author 1330–1400

David McCullough, *1776*, Simon and Schuster, 2005

John Gunther, *Inside U.S.A.*, 1947

Jung Chang, *Mao: The Unknown Story*, Anchor Books, 2005

Geert Hofstede, *Cultures and Organizations*, McGraw Hill, 2010

Weijian Shan, *Out of the Gobi: My Story of China and America*, Wiley, 2019

Nicole Perlroth, *This Is How They Tell Me the World Ends*, Bloomsbury, 2021

Richard Haass, *The World: A Brief Introduction*, Penguin, 2020

Donald Calman, *The Nature and Origins of Japanese Imperialism*, Routledge, 1992

Sterling and Peggy Seagrave, *The Yamato Dynasty*, Broadway Books, 1999

Acknowledgements

I received the best of all possible schooling at Le Rosey School in Switzerland where I made some of my closest friends that include Michael Korda, Christian Delsol, and Harold de Wolff. Unfortunately, others suffer from poor health and some have passed away. My education proceeded at Princeton University where Peter Jefferys and I became friends for life. My dear friend Alvin Cramer Segal from Irving School days became a hugely successful businessman in Canada.

My own parents contributed so much to my personal culture, feeling for and knowledge of languages and a sense that the entire world matters. My mother is honored in her life story, *Dottie*, my first published book. My father, and separately my stepfather, gave me so much knowledge, affection, and life experience, right on a silver platter.

I am a self-made man. The story of my life is written in detail in my autobiography, *Eiertanz*. No single person gave me advancement, but my bosses and colleagues at Citibank, at Schroders, at Private investment Company for Asia, and at Swiss Bank Corporation were supporters and teachers, and some were examples.

Friends like Makoto Yasuda, Robert Hirst, Richard Margolis, David Gemmill, Major Mick Stanley, Pierre Lavie, and my much loved mentor the late Henry Arnhold all contributed.

This book is largely drawn from my own life and knowledge, experience, and personal culture. Although here and there, I checked facts on the Internet, there is nothing in this book that is inspired by or drawn from any specific reading.

Good or bad, it comes out of my own head.

I'm deeply grateful to my wife, Barbara Spakowski Wodtke, for her brilliant mind, vast cultural reach, deep knowledge of Asia and Europe, unstinting love, and constant encouragement.

Rick Wolff, Senior Executive Editor-at-Large, from Kevin Anderson & Associates, did a terrific job advising me on points that needed to be expressed more clearly and important issues that deserved greater detail. Rick reminded me that there is sensitivity to matters involving political correctness and that persons such as university presidents must cope with such matters in their work on a daily basis, while I have the luxury of criticism.

Fran Keilty of Hickory Stick Bookshop in Washington, Connecticut, believed in me and offered me a book signing in 2021 and a second book signing in December 2022.

This is now the third book that will be overseen and published through my friend Louise Johnson and her colleagues at Katart, in New Milford, Connecticut. Always up to the mark in sensing the correct way to go and in matters of good practice in publishing, Louise and Art Foote are used to me and never get upset when I say:

"There is no hurry; any time in the next thirty seconds will be fine."

Peter G. Wodtke   **October 25, 2022**

Made in the USA
Middletown, DE
28 November 2022

15915571R00136